Words of Wisdom

To reach safe haven forever you must be found to be just like

- Me -

by

Scott Beemer

The Tennessee Publishing House
496 Mountain View Drive
Mosheim, TN 37818-3524

Words of Wisdom

To reach safe haven forever you must be found to be just like

- Me -

by

Scott Beemer

Published in the United States
By
The Tennessee Publishing House
Mosheim, Tennessee March 2010
First Edition, First Printing

Cover Design: Kellie Warren-Underwood

Disclaimer:

This document is an original work of the author. It may include reference to information commonly known or freely available to the general public. Any resemblance to other published information is purely coincidental. The author has in no way attempted to use material not of his own original unless such information has been cited, documented or given some other properly recognized written form of credit for such work The Tennessee Publishing House disclaims any association with or responsibility for the ideas, opinions or facts as expressed by the author of this book.

**Printed in the Unites States of America
Cataloging-in-Publication
ISBN: 978-1-58275-218-1 Paperback
Copyright March 2010 by Scott Beemer
ALL RIGHTS RESERVED**

WORDS of WISDOM

*To reach safe haven forever you
must be found to be just like ME.*

*So walk with Me wherever you
go, and you will
have the ongoing blessings of
Our eternity together.*

ACKNOWLEDGEMENTS

The Holy Spirit inspired this entire book as it was received by Scott Beemer and Jean Beemer in their morning devotions.

PROLOGUE

PLACE OF BALANCE

This Holy Bible that I have given to My children is My way of introduction into the world of the Spirit. This Spirit world is My place of ALL of forever! (John 3:33-36) It is a place of truth, only truth! (John 4:23,24) What is true truth? It is only what I show My children. Anything not of true truth is only the underside of all things. This "underside" is only the opposite of good. All My things are only of good. Balance in all things requires that both sides be real, but the reality of all things does not have to be open and made alive in My realm.

If there were no darkness how would light show forth? If there is a top side there must be a bottom. In My Spirit realm only light is shown but darkness must stay and keep light the balance! (Rev. 22:5; 21:22-25) This, My dear ones, is very reasonable for the perfect balance brings perfection of desire. To reach

My place of balance is your way of Spirit growth. To reach safe haven forever you must be found to be just like Me! (John 15:4,5; I Cor. 15:28; Eph.1:22,23; Eph.2:22; Eph.3:9; 19; Eph. 4:21-25; Col. 1;20)

WORDS OF WISDOM

LOVE'S GOAL

These days are growing more desirable as We grow closer. This time is becoming a walk of wonders, privileges, and joy. Just a closer walk with Me, is your goal to be obtained! Just believe to achieve. Your goal is the bridge to your forever place with Me, so keep the flow ever ongoing. In words I build new areas of works and wonders. Just be more aware of words of wonder, and the great wonder of words. Kingdoms and castles, hills and mountains, lakes, seas, and waters of works beyond the heavens all are to grow, expand, and increase man's delight! There is no end to all I have, and endless is the joy and delight I bring to My children. No sight or view is given yet of heaven's great expansion, showing slowly the revelation of My blessings waiting for My children. All of this is love's goal!

There is time enough, time for work, time to pray, and time to spend with Me. Our time together is so important to your Spiritual growth. Be aware of My presence, talk to Me as you would another person, and then listen as I talk to you. Hear with your inner ear what I am saying to you. Know the message of Love, the direction for your life, the encouraging thoughts I have for you. *"Be still and know that I am God."* In the stillness We are One. In stillness you should and will know My presence and I am for you. I am your Father God, and you are My beloved children created to be with Me always, My love will cover you always. Remember: *"Draw neigh to God, and He will draw neigh to you,"* this is My promise to you.

MY DELIGHT

To My delight I bring to light many desires of My heart! I am saying these things long held back but deemed right and worthy of release. My children have great needs, and by_their attention paid to what I say, many will to be more pleasing to Me than if left as before! It is good to air out such as We are touching on. I let good flow when proper interest rises up My children to seek more and more. My delight is in seeing My children grow closer in Spiritual knowledge and wisdom. All will eventually come to this exposure of My truths flowing, but what a blessing to release some new truths daily to lead, guide, encourage, and lift up all who rise to seek more! This word pouring out here is bringing enlightenment and blessings to many who otherwise might be set in another place!

Be content and thankful that God is supplying all your needs. Actually He even promises: *"Delight thyself in the Lord and He shall give thee the desires of thine heart."* God wants you to live an abundant life. Having an abundant life you are able to help others, to supply where there is need. "See a need and fill it" becomes possible in and abundant life. Constantly praise and thank your Lord for the blessings, of the abundant life you enjoy. Be a channel of these blessings to others that are in need. Be a blessing, encouraging others as you go through the days. Have a smile on your face, and that lets them know you love them, and so does God. Be a channel of God's love to others. This will bring the joy of the Lord and strength from the Father.

The careful reviewing of the things you have been reading here will always bring blessings and rewards. My blessings flow when hearts are lighted truth. Keep your eyes on and looking for truth. Only truth, My truth shows love, My love as I desire it to be. All seeking must be controlled to dwell on truth, My truth. Man seeking elsewhere on earth can open up much to his own detriment! This is a trap set by Satan and many a man has been lost just by seeking things that interest him not Me. Earth life lived for Me requires a walk holding My hand of guidance. **This is a warning for care to be taken when delving into things of the Holy Spirit** when still in an earth suit of flesh!

Be an over-comer! Every day rise above the problems and stumbling blocks that come your way. Keep your eyes on Jesus, knowing that He is lifting you up above the worldly trials before you. Face each problem before you and walk right through it, trusting the Lord to see you through. You were created by God to be a victor in every situation. Your God will make a way for you. You are to go forward, trusting the Lord in all your ways.

TRUTH JUST TRUTH

The times have been set in My word by Me, and I intend to see to their unfolding in truth just as I have said and recorded. Truth will come to My dear ones who believe, see that it is only My truth that you believe. Many are the imaginations of man, but My children shall understand Truth in all its clarity. Hearts that are Mine have heads that are Mine! No child of Mine harbors untruth and follows that. How else can peace be harbored except in truth? Not all pulpits send truth forth, so I expect truth to be in the heads and hearts of true believers! Let not untruth find a place in your heart. Ask Me and I will answer, seek Me and you will find. Only truth in clarity is truth in fact! Seek the facts of truth and you will find Me! I am truth all truth all of the time!

God's love for His children is everlasting and powerful. It will protect from harm, it will provide guidance, and it will sustain you in any situation. It is available for all who will look to Jesus and invite Him into their hearts. God sacrificed His only Son, and Jesus willingly went to the cross and died, so that our sins would be washed away by the blood of Jesus. We have been cleansed and made whole through His death. Have an abundantly thankful heart. Walk daily with Him, praise Him, and worship Him. Be the child of God He wants you to be. Jesus made it all possible on the cross at Calvary!

SEEKERS

The unraveling of truth from man's fiction requires My hand of careful selection! Some truths told in error or with blemishes have kept a covering of evil alive to disrupt and confuse the casual seeker. After all am I to be sought casually or just when time permits? This time of "sometime seeking" is going to be exposed in an explosion of My truths! All My children in whom I've put My Spirit are to be shaken and awakened to Me as truth is revealed! Yes, this is the end time blessing not yet told, but I am now stating the truth of truth only. Truth should now be released from My true truth teachers! Entry is only given in truth to true truth seekers. Isn't this reasonable? Jesus is truth; Jesus in the hearts of true truth seekers can only release Jesus in truth! Tear down confusion for what it is, a losing path for the casual seeker. All seekers are not My truth discerners! See that truth in words and in deeds becomes your banner exposed! Yes, truth should be the honey sweet and most attractive to those hungry for Me in truth!

Take time to worship and praise the Lord. In the quiet time seek His Face and experience His presence in your life. *"Draw neigh to God, and He will draw neigh to you."* As you surround yourself with His presence, and His glory, He will lift you up, strengthen you, and fill you with the righteousness of God. Live in His righteousness. *"Surely goodness and mercy will follow you all the days of your life."* As you walk with Him His love covers you, for you are a child of God.

DAILY SEEKING

It is with daily seeking I find My loved ones who love Me. This is truth in action that I can watch over, lead, and care for. All My children do I can watch over and guide, when they are doing the things I direct and I am pleased with. To follow Me identifies the ones I can watch over, lead and guide. I seek to help all My children, but I help most those who find My guidance, and then seek more and more. I favor those who are listening and doing. Those who just read and read My word but do nothing I've said are useless in My Kingdom. Only hearers and then doers are setting themselves in the path I can lead and guide them. Seek My will and do My will, and then your hope has a great foundation I can build upon.

Dedicate your life to Jesus and His word. Live according to the Scriptures, for this is God's plan for you. His plan is one of love, and of Spiritual growth. By His plan, His way, you are lifted up and drawn into a closer walk with Him. Seek to know His way for it leads to happiness and a peace that passes understanding. Live your life in peace for in this manner the Lord can touch you with His love and rejoice for you are a beloved child of God. His blessings cover you always.

PERSISTENT TRUTH

It is with persistence I build My Kingdom, and it is with persistence My children will find their place with Me. See that this persistence is persistent in truth, for truth, and about truth, and then truth will surround and secure those who are true truth seekers! Jesus is truth, and it is though the searching or truth that the true children of God are identified! See that this is clear in all the hearts of My seeking ones, for this is the method of sure identification that I seek for and wait for! Only in truth is anything built that is worthwhile! Pray now that this truth shall be made known as I am made known. Truth is the rocks of all the foundations of worth, see how obvious truth should be? Who can truly trust anything if truth isn't a shining light exposing its self? Is there a Heaven? Is there a Hell? Where does truth lie?

"Many are the afflictions of the righteous, but the Lord delivereth him out of them all." Walk in the way I have set before you. Let your praise and worship be in your prayer. Have a thankful heart. Remember God's word for you, *"But the salvation of the righteous is of the Lord: He is their strength in time of trouble."* You are constantly being strengthened as you walk with Him. His healing power is upon you now and forever.

His Love overcomes all things. Draw neigh to Lord and He will take care of you. Trust in your Lord; know that His mercy endures forever!

SEEK IN TRUTH

When I call a man and that man listens and hears, then I expect him to seek and search for truth only My truth. Nothing else is worthwhile! I build all I have based only on truth, and in truth all things will come about. This truth should be a hunger in every child of Mine, for only then can peace and comfort I give come forth in ultimate satisfaction! Without truth everything would be built on a foundation of sand! Come now dear ones and seek Me in truth and I will be found, then We shall be as One, for only in truth do I dwell in My fullness! My glory only bursts forth as truth is made real in the hearts of My children. My love only flows in the heart of truth. The heavens that I hold up in display every night, are only showing truth in My reality! I have made a display of truth in reality by My empty tomb. Come dear ones seek only truth from My Bible and find all about Me!

You are being protected by the loving hand of God. *"For He shall give His angels charge over thee, to keep thee in all thy ways."* God's love for His created children is powerful and everlasting. It is His desire that we return that love. God says, *"Because he hath set his love upon me, therefore will I deliver him. I will set him on high because he hath known my name."* Call upon the name of the Lord, rest in His love, know and return His great love. He is watching over you, desiring a closer walk. He hears your prayers and is always working for your good.

TRUE TRUTH

In all My time with man have I sought to bring him out only with truth? What would be the purpose with any other approach? But in the earth home of man roams an adversary of devious ways. His attack is through lies. Lies are a distortion or a confusion of truth! In all My teachers I seek to draw out only truth, but true truth is hard to depict when subtleties and innuendos invade and permeate the air with their mistruths causing great confusion. I use this distraction as a tool to weed out the unworthy, insincere, and useless ones. How else can true truth seekers **become** unless there is this bed of confusion for them to come forth from? These end times are becoming an example of a climax of obstruction, misdirection, and misguidance. I am using all of this now as a quick discerner of those I seek, desire, and search for! Seek only truth in these last days and I will draw you close to Me all of the time. Make self dethroned your goal of the present, and your love for Jesus will be shown by seeking in truth! All truth flows freely as My children set their feet in the path I open to them!

The glory of the Lord shines forth. It covers our world and surrounds each of His children. Lift up your prayers to the Father, in the name of Jesus, for He is listening for you. Send praises and worship, know that God hears every word directed to Him. He is answering your prayers, and always working for your good. Trust in Him, in His word and promises, for He is ever faithful. God's love is forever. He created you to be a child of God. He gave you free will to choose, to love Him or the world and self. Who will you choose? *"For God so loved the world that He gave His only begotten Son, That whosoever believeth in Him shall not perish but have everlasting life.*" God is love! Walk in His way of love!

SEARCH FOR TRUTH

Search diligently for truth and true truth will appear. Only to clean hearts and sincere ones will I cause their eyes to open and their way to be made sure. I set before all I bring before you these truths here revealed, and teach all those whose ears are open to My truth, will, and way. For only those dear ones can I trust, teach, lead, and guide. Nothing has changed in man unless man allows, seeks, desires and submits to Me his all, then We will have the times released of true walks, and true wonders with truth flowing as water from an endless spout! Give this search for truth all the time and all the effort required by Me, for this is the path to My heart always!

See yourself as being free, free from the constraints of fear, anger, or hate. Cast away any negative thoughts and release the glory of God into your life. Let all thoughts be covered by love and peace. Remember that

Jesus has come into your heart and you have been changed. Constantly think God thoughts, thoughts of love and goodness toward others and toward yourself. You are a child of God. He is watching over you and leading you into His righteousness. Enjoy the peace that He brings into your life. Seek the face of Jesus and be filled with His goodness and His love. It is available to you, receive all God has for you. Live in peace.

LOVE FOR JESUS

The people's love of self has set all people apart from God. This must be made clear to Our loved ones especially at this close of age. Teach the love for Jesus, this is the way for this separation from self! Yes, all My children should have a clear picture of the great necessity of this separation. The times are demanding this move to be made clear! The love for Jesus is like a healing balm covering the heart with His love of protection making all things required to be easy to accomplish! Before this has always been left to the individual growth, a rather haphazard way to do it! But now spread this word, "I will help everyone who hears and tries his best to obey." This is an especially important word for Now! The children of this age have more distractions than ever before so this extra help is most needed! Yes, put this out for all to see, hear and then obey!

Walk each day in the righteousness of the Lord. Take of His peace, of His strength, and of His wisdom. The Bible tells you to *"Trust in the Lord with all your heart: and all your ways acknowledge Him, and He shall direct your path."* Also *"Seek ye first the kingdom of God and His righteousness, and all these things shall be added unto you."* Put God first in all things and you shall be blessed.

MY WORDS

Never see My words as tiresome or as unworthy; for it is by My words I established the heavens and the earth! When I speak to My children, it is always for their good. Whether I speak good or evil always depends on them. Evil spoken should instruct and bring lessons of worth just as the good I say. All My words have purpose or I would not bother. See that all My words are so honored! These books We have done, and are doing, should be properly regarded! I have a worthy purpose for them! The timing is My timing, and I am watching over all of this carefully. This today is to encourage and reassure all who read this that I truly have a plan and a time of release! So read carefully all that is here given, I make this a comfort and a blessing to all!

"Peace I leave with you, my peace I give unto you; not as the world gives, give I unto you. Let not your heart be troubled, neither let it be afraid." For surely I am with you always My love is everlasting. Look to Me for all things. Look to Me in confidence, knowing and believing that I am answering your prayers. Remember: *"But my God shall supply all your needs according to His riches in glory by Christ Jesus."* This scripture is God's promise to His people. Have peace in your heart and soul, and lean on His Word. He is faithful and filled with love and grace toward His children.

MY WORKS

All efforts to seek more of Me and My works must be controlled as I wish, so only truth that helps growth will be given. That is why I do things that seem confusing, it is only to bring Truth that is timely and helpful for the people, time, or place. To grow properly for one may not fit or be helpful for another. There are problems that teaching groups of people the same thing encounter. This business of teaching truth has many obstacles to be overcome. Here is the truth of trying to spread truth to all My children. Sometimes, truth shown in books gives the seekers the opportunity to grow at a pace more suitable for them. This is another reason for books to be slow in growing! I will have My way, just when is hard to say, so I must just end My efforts sometime cutting off slow growers and lack of achievers. To push slow and steady until each one is ready never will bring everyone to the same place of perfection, but will satisfy the most!

"I am come that they might have life and that they might have it more abundantly!" Walk in the abundant life God is providing for you. You are His blessed child. His mercy endureth forever as does His grace toward His children. Seek the face of Jesus, Look to Him in all things. *"Delight thyself in the Lord and He shall give thee the desires*

of thine heart." Enjoy the fellowship you have with the Lord. Each day try to walk closer to Him, and appreciate Him more. Let His glorious Love be your covering. Be you strengthened as you wait upon the Lord, for truly He is your strength.

TRUE LOVE

Only I can bring unity and togetherness in and among My children. It is through time given, and properly used, that My children will grow closer to Me as I desire. The True tug of unity is My drawing power of love, that's why Oneness is slow growing. I am slow in giving true love. **True love is a badge of security meant for all eternity.** Can you now see why true love seems distant and hard to obtain? Children in the flesh are only chosen as "likely candidates;" these are My children who are more carefully watched over and guided. They are chosen only because of their great desire to gain love, My love. All true growing power in the Spirit is controlled by "true love's guidance." True love cannot be forced, coerced, or demanded, it only flows as love is desired in true hearts. True hearts are born by true desire growing in seeking truth. Jesus is truth!

We have this heavenly connection; you are the branch and I am the tree. The branch is a part of the tree. Therefore, if the tree is an apple tree, the branch will produce apples. If there is no fruit produced the branch must be cut off. Are you bearing fruit in your daily life? Does Christ show forth in your life? You are a Christian do others know you are a Christian by your action, or your life style? Truly, they will know you are Christian by your love. God is love; therefore, His children must be filled with love. Just as an apple tree produces apples, the children of God should reflect the love of the Lord.

FOREVER PLAN

Yes, I Cor. 15:45-49 has in it the true picture of My children for eternity. As I have said, "I change not." My first plan for man is just as the plan I now intend to pursue! Isn't it clear? In Adam on earth I made man a soul, and then in Christ I made man a Spirit. This is the original plan, and it is My ongoing forever plan! Earth truly is the birth place of My children, first a soul, then a Spirit! Evil came and I have used it for good, to weed out the unusable, the unworthy, and the unwanted; I then have a pure cleansed source forever to raise My family of forever! Give this deep thought, for is this lies My truth forever!

Look up and seek the face of Jesus. Have the mind of Jesus. Desire that His will be done in your life. Be a willing vessel, always available. Remember: *"I can do all things through Christ which strengtheth me."* You are filled with the Holy Spirit, God's Spirit. The fruit of this Spirit is available to you; love, peace, joy, patience, gentleness, goodness, faith, meekness, and self control against such there is no law. Allow these blessings from God to be developed in you. Call on them. Thank God for blessing you and supplying all your needs.

PURSUIT OF TRUTH

This pursuit of truth is really never ending! All truth is God which no man, even a rejuvenated one, will ever come to knowing "all truth." However, the constant pursuit in sincerity will open worlds of heaven spilling forth truth forevermore. Seeking My desires, purposes, dreams, and hopes becomes an endless journey of wonders that no man in the flesh will ever comprehend. The truth pursuing is the right and only path worthwhile, so seek and follow as I lead for great times ahead! Keep grounded in the Holy Bible for from there I can open the mysteries and wonders for man in the flesh. Keep this pursuit up for it pleases the Father and the Son. Yes, I have many plans and ideas that I can open about where we can go and what we can do together. Many are the ways of growth for man not yet opened up, but this also needs to be looked into. Many paths beneficial to man's understanding are still to be shown as man in flesh grows more as I desire. This is part of the 1000 year's task, as you are learning man in the flesh is ever ongoing!

Go forward constantly for I am with you, My strength is your strength. *"The joy of the Lord is your strength,"* You have been redeemed by the blood of Jesus so all things are possible. I am with you and I hear your prayers. Have faith in My words for they are for you, My children. Walk boldly for you are not alone. *"As the Father hath loved me, so have I loved you: continue ye in my love."*

TREASURES OF LOVE

The pursuit of truth is never ending, and this is always to your advantage. Hope, hope alive forevermore. Yes, this is a beautiful part of your future, as are you now, eager and seeking truth, so shall you ever be, for My Kingdom is endless, and My mysteries are always ongoing! What a blessing will come forth from everlasting to everlasting. Happiness and joy are centered in the ongoing newness of forever. Could such a thing be? Yes, of course, for I am your source unstoppable, never ending. Love moving and flowing is always ongoing. Keep your mind filled with My truths to know My all ongoing treasures of love unfolding! Am I not showing you the heavens above more and more? Does it not conjure up the thoughts of My beauty unfolding? Is not My slow revelation of the wonders above a proof of what I am now saying?

The time has come for new things; renewed faith, newness in your love for others, more patience and kindness, more consideration one for another. I would have you desire

Oneness with the Father, that you would have a passion for more of Him, His love and peace filling you. *"Arise, shine, for thy light is come, and the glory of the Lord is risen upon thee,"* Let this scripture be true in your life. Truly the glory of the Lord is upon God's children as they seek more of Him.

MY RECORD

Make an effort to make each day a milestone of record showing your steady progress toward the goal of Mine that has been set in your heart! In this manner you and I will be able to show others this proof of Our works. Truly no work of Mine should be done with. Have I not shown you My record plainly in My Bible? Proof of My desires are plainly recorded, and it is good that there be proof of your walk, will, and way also! My children grow stronger as they fulfill My plan for them, how else can I be sure of what is done on Our behalf. Yes, a trail of record, success or failure, is important for many reasons. First man must be plainly shown how I desire to work. Doesn't My Bible show that plain enough? You too should able to show your record of worth or failure for both reveals your trail of growth!

Be confident in all you do when you know I'm by your side.

Rise up and glorify the Lord. He is your source of all things; peace, love, health, and walking in the joy of His blessings to you. Be ye lifted up in Spirit. Be covered in body, soul, and Spirit by His everlasting love. Let your mind be renewed as He blesses you. Feel His peace wash over you as His renewing power is your covering. Walk in this manner daily letting His light shine forth and light the way for you and for others. Be a beacon of God's light for truly that is God's will for you.

TRUE PURPOSES

Yes, these days are days of revelation, a time for My desired knowledge to be brought forth. Seek after and follow scriptures as I reveal through them My will and way, My true purposes for these last days. Wake up, stir up, and lift up My dear ones who are lacking that that I desire, for these times. Words of Mine flow steady and true to touch hearts and minds of those who are My true truth seekers. Do the things that I ask, **follow the way that I lead. Do not hold back that that I am revealing!**

Truly when My children listen and hear from Me, I pour out My love through words that they may learn to listen and hear more and more. I am an endless well where every child is encouraged to dip buckets of wisdom and barrels of love. Tell My stories, tell My love, tell all who will listen or read with love! Hearing with ears in your head to things I have said will open your heart's ears to hear heaven's truths poured out. To listen in your heart gives heavenly wisdom a chance to grow, filling you with truth you're to know. Growing closer every day is My desire for all who seek truth's true way. Continue in all I set before you, and do with sure knowing you are on the path I've called you to. Keep daily progress for this work will be used!

Say, here I am, available for an infilling of your righteousness, your wisdom, and love. My child, walk each day in harmony with others knowing that you are a child of God. Step out, confidently able to do all things I have put before you. *"I am the vine, you are the branch."* Draw strength and direction from Me. Go forth the way I have set before you. As long as We are connected in the Spirit you will be able to do My will. Always have an attitude of love, of peace, and let the joy of the Lord flood your soul. In this manner I can direct you into My way. Receive the righteousness I have for you, and you will be lifted up. Know that My mercy endures forever and My love is covering My children.

THIS WORK

This work We are doing runs the gamut from here to there, this is good to be free in what We come together in, but these last times need to zero in on what the Father cares about most. That is the condition of the Bride in these times. Where are all My children going? Why do I not see more coming to Our table every morning? Truly more of My children should be working bringing more of My children to My table. Talk about this more to those who will listen, tell them how short the time is, and how few are coming to Me for salvation! Yes, read My books, teach My dear ones, and seek My lost ones! Why not you? There are so few!

Thy will be done in me and through me, oh Lord my strength and my redeemer. Be still and know that I am God. Listen to My still soft voice, and learn of the blessings I have for you. Know that My presence is always about you bringing love and protection into your life. Go forth boldly in My name. Remember: *"I can do all things through Christ which strengtheth me,"* is My promise to you. Let others see Jesus in you. Let this love, My love, flow to all others. *"Freely you have received, freely, freely give!"* Give of the blessings from the Lord, be an open channel so that God may use you to reach others. Go forth for *"The joy of the Lord is my strength."*

LISTEN

I pour forth in words true and truth see that this flow continues in the hearts of more and more of My children. Only My words of individual direction will lead them where their best place dwells with Me. Make this cry of Mine get to the hearts who will listen! Only My last words of direction now will lead many to their true place with Me. Come now and let My truth ring out into hearts ready for harvest! Yes, this is the time for words of harvest to be used for the proper work to be done! **Who will listen who will care? Only hearts I prepare! Heed this call, send this word, all of this should be heard!**

"Arise, shine, for thy light has come, and the glory of the Lord is risen upon thee." Yes, My child arise, for I am with you, My strength is your strength. You are being directed by the Holy Spirit within. Go forth boldly and I will lead you into situations where you can be a blessing. Release the fruit of the Holy Spirit into your life and all things will become possible. *"Let not your Heart be troubled,"* but go forth confidently because I am with you always.

HEAR AND DO

Yes, I do pour forth truth more and more, but only to those whose hearts retain and obey the things I say. Hearing is as a great work My children can do! When I speak, and words are few, then listen more for what you should do. I speak to few for many pretend, and seldom do! My love given is pure and true, so should be the things you show, so follow up, learn to do! My words are pure and true and so should be the things you do! Follow Me, and My will should lead, giving worth to all who heed! I send words to grow and create, making desires satisfy Me. My desires should be your desires as I find children I can inspire. To be filled with things I know, can lead My children to obey and show!

In this time of earthly troubles stand fast, for I am with you. Continue to be a light of the Lord, steadfast and patient. Let My love set your attitude. Be ye filled with peace and love one for another. Let gentleness come forth and meekness cover your soul. Have perfect faith that My presence is about you, Remember: *"Thou will keep him in perfect peace, whose mind is stayed on Thee, because he trusteth in thee."* Release the God given fruit of the Holy Spirit into your life and you will have the self-control needed. Let love cover all and the Joy of the lord will be yours.

THE WALK

Our walk grows weeds as you wander from the things I say. Learn self-control to hear, listen, and obey. Your hearing is fruitful when your listening causes you to be obedient to what I say! Only this way will bring spring out of winter. All obedience To My will and way lifts the listener to truth closer into My arms. Consider not the amount of time spent listening, only hearing then obeying counts! These words today are avenues of joy when obedience is the plate you eat from. Picking fruit from the tree of life still requires the peeling, slicing, and eating to enjoy the worth of your effort. My children's hunger should cause them to desire fruit from the top to the bottom of this tree!

OUR EFFORTS

The worth of Our efforts shows only in the doing of that I allow. With great care do the works of Our efforts, guarding carefully the truths that unfold. Know full well that which you say and do should also be all that I have allowed. Never go too far when it is just building up your self esteem, for I hold that in little regard. Carefully walk this walk We are on, and then will its fruit drop from the tree of its birth ready and ripe for the work assigned it! All this that I say today should be saved, thought about, used and considered carefully so that victory will ring clear as a bell sounding in beauty! **I give you these words today, do not be foolish and turn away!** Do not, or dwell not, on what the foolish do, dwell only on the things I give to you. To follow self is a confusing task, leading one to Satan's mask.

MY SPACE

This consistency of reading and doing is building roads, bridges, and highways from earth into space. My space is where I open heavens that no man can view. Only children, My children, who have passed My tests, and seek only My goals, have special passes required that only I give. These passes for eternity are delving into kingdoms of My choosing. I open this door now for a peek into hope's chest full of dreams. Yes, I have all these kinds of things that are not dreams! My reality still is before you; but by these words I can lift the veil I control bringing truths of Mine to entice and draw more and more children of worth out of the physical reality into Our Spiritual truths of forever. You truly have a Spiritual space and place to occupy. My heaven in heaven right now is also an in between place I hold children "in work." Fresh from earth into "Spirit" is shock enough to start, but I'm saying until the end of the 1000 years, all My family are still "in between." When My plan is free of evils entanglement (no more death or Satan); then will I be free to open eyes to true truths of space and space's places that Hubble is showing.

The time is come to rest completely in the Lord. He has created you and fashioned you to be a child of God. He has equipped you with everything necessary to live a Godly, righteous life. You have the Holy Spirit with all of His power you have the fruit of the Spirit which truly makes you an over-comer. Use these blessings in your life that your life may be full. Let His presence, and His love be your constant covering, and all else will be made possible!

ONE HEART

The working of the thought processes of man's mind bears answers of his heart and mind, but the thinking that should come from man's heart gives guidance which I start. My children must start giving more thought to listening in their heart for Me.

Only then do I give the attention that comes from My heart. Our hearts are to be One, how else can Our togetherness grow? True teaching comes only in this manner. Until I release man's will and way to follow and seek after My truths he is allowed to search only what he thinks he should know. This is being led by man's head [soul] not by his God given wisdom. Spiritual growth is an area where I must have control and give guidance! Teach the children to seek Me more in the Spirit and truth this is their way to have My guidance from Me! (John 4:23,24)

No man comes to the Father but through Jesus, His Son. Jesus is the light of the world, there is no darkness in Him. You are to seek after the light, and flee from the darkness. Take on the light of the Lord, walk in it, let your light (God's light) so shine that others may see it and know that Jesus is Lord. Let all your thoughts and actions be a reflection of Jesus in you. Have joy in the knowledge of the Lord. Strength comes for, *"The joy of the Lord is my strength."* Rest; be in peace, for you are a child of God. He is watching over you in love. Let His peace fill your heart!

The call has been put out during all of these last days, but few are My children who listen, hear, and obey. How am I to shape those who won't pay attention? All you can do is all I ask you to do. I speak now straight to the heart of those who are reading what is here written. To read these words will give great favor and blessings or they will be used to condemn and set straight the rights I give and the "readers only" have dismissed. Words save and build up or condemn and separate. How else can there be victors and losers? I don't make losers, I make winners. Losers embrace selfishness and laziness doing their own thing or just what is easiest. Where are you who are now reading My words, My Bible, and or listening to your own heart's way? Set your feet on the path I have opened for soon, so soon, this door will close! Truth poured forth becomes a great separator, dividing and proving all children with great surety!

Soon you will go home to be with the Lord, but now is the time to draw closer to Him. Spend more time with Him. Know of Jesus and His love through the scriptures. Be ye lifted up and made joyful in His love and grace. Be confident that you are a child of God, let His will be done in your life. Continue to be in prayer and praise for the Lord hears you prayers. Let praise continually be on your lips and in your heart. Continue to release the blessings of the fruit of the Spirit into your life. Let your life be a reflection of Jesus, filled with His love, peace, and joy. Rise up in faith and show the Lord for He is your strength, He will show the way. His love is your covering!

TRUST AND CONFIDINCE

When things are confusing and not going your way, wait have faith, for I am with you. Lean on Me, rest in Me, and I will carry you. These are the times of testing and trying. No one comes to Me in their own strength. If you tried it would not impress Me, for it would show lack of knowledge and trust! Together We are strong, alone you are wrong. These are times of trust and confidence growing! Seek My peace draw closer, rest in My comfort! All of Our things will unfold on time and in My perfection.

Togetherness is a gift for hard times, use it for all that is intended! I make all things new, but only in the perfection of My times. Hurry up and wait is another way of running ahead and then not seeing! All things should flow in My way to go. Rise up and be the child of God I have created you to be. Focus your thinking on the Lord Jesus and His will for you always. Have the mind of Christ and you live in peace. Speak the words of faith, speak the Scriptures which are God's blessings for you. Believe His Word is true, and as if it was written just for you. God's love and peace are enfolding you as long as you choose to abide with Him. He is with you. Are you with Him?

MY WAYS

When I show My things to My loved ones I will make My way known plain and simple. Do not be caught up in any complex or complicated scheme of things! Plain is My way and simple are the paths I open to My loved ones. I do not call you children for no good reason. My ways are far above your ways in the flesh, but you are called to much more than this earth and flesh you now know! Yes, you are now children in My sight but you are much more in My heart! Soon enough the Spirit realm will be your home, and then We will be as One together in all My things. It's your heart that is in preparation now so your soul will grow. My plan is your perfection, have I not called you Gods? (John 10:34)

Be a champion, be the winner I have created you to be. Remember: I have put within you the Holy Spirit and His power and blessings for your use. Release into your life these blessings, use them and develop them for the glory of God. See others with more understanding and compassion. Be thankful to the loving God who is watching over you. Rise up in Spirit and the body will follow. Have the mind of Christ filled with joy. Live each day with an attitude of joy and peace, for this is yours through the fruit of the Holy Spirit. Make manifest in your life the blessings that have been imparted to you!

MY DESIRES

In the world I have laid My hope for I have a plan, a plan for man to become My true children of forever. Yes, to be My inheritance throughout time. Far above their earthly thoughts shall they arise! Yes, My sons and daughters, My kingdom- makers, for them I am preparing all of the heavens for their pleasures forevermore; a universe for eternity to expand, build and grow, yes beauty beyond all belief, love within their reach. truth expanding into My desires and purposes as I please! We are One, in My image, I have expanded My Self as family for all to know, and grow, sowing the all I sow!

Sowing

Simply sow, all is known
All is seen, all is sown.
Hearts expand all I see
Seeking rewards all shall be.
Never doubt, believe in all,
See results to all I call.

Cast your cares on the Lord for He cares for you. *"Trust in the Lord with all your heart, lean not on your own understanding. In all your ways acknowledge Him and He shall direct your path."* My child, walk the path I have prepared for you. My way is the way, the only way for you. My way is the way of love, of peace, and of growing in grace.

Have a gentle and loving heart full of patience and understanding. See others through the eyes of Jesus. *"Let not your heart be troubled for I am with you."* Persevere in this life's walk for it is Our training ground and much is being accomplished in the Spirit. Lift up your head and praise the Lord!

FREELY DRAW YOURSELF

When I set a plan for man I dictate or control not that man, but I let his will and way either draw him into that plan or not! My plans are Godly plans and I require that man, each by himself, draw himself freely and willingly into harmony with My desires. Man must be moved in his Spirit and soul to attain to working freely with Me in the Holy Spirit. This then sets a man to freely be My child in the place I desire for him. This why men are mostly slow in reaching the place I have set to be his. Can you now see why so few truly attain to the high positions I would hold out for each one? Yes, freely, freely, come to My place I have for you, freely, freely, you will attain. No high position is given by Me in any way! All who would be best must be best early in their own hearts, then I am able to assist and draw them higher and higher!

"Draw nigh to God, and He will draw nigh to you." In prayer, in praise you are close to God, then you are to listen to what He has to say to you. Close your mind to earthly thoughts and hear what the Lord is saying to you. You are His created child and He loves you and wants to guide you and lift you up. Be receptive to God's will for you. Have an open heart, always willing to hear and obey. He wants a close walk with you. Pray, praise, listen, and hear His voice.

THE WORK

When I call a man I then will prepare him for the task that I require. I call only those who have prepared themselves enough to be worthy of My calling. See how there must be already a working in the soul and Spirit of a man before I find him useful for My purposes. As the self is controlled by man, then I can find a man I can use to fill My desires. It follows then that that man must learn to follow Me until that self is ignored, then gone completely, for I will take the self that is not used! *"Thy Word is health unto my bones.*" Thy Word I deposit in my heart, and I believe it is just for me from my Father. I will speak words of faith regardless of the circumstances. I will stand on the Words of Jesus. *"By His stripes ye were healed." "I have come that they might have life, and that they have it more abundantly."* I have an abundant and healed life because of Jesus and His Word. I believe! Our Father is a loving God, watching over His children. Rest in Him and be restored by His love.

WORTHY ONES

By man's persistence in seeking truth that man is identified by Me as My worthy child. Seek not the foolishness of the world, but seek the things of the Spirit not shown. This searching heart I watch over, lead, and guide, yet they know Me not! My dear ones I am Spirit and My gift to man is everlasting life, but what that means is yet to be made clear or manifested! I draw the worthy ones until their heart is awakened to hear Me in their Spirit! This then is what is meant when Jesus said, **unless the Father draws them. My way draws man into the Spirit realm slowly and carefully.** Only then can Our working together closely take place. Think it not strange when My children do things man does not readily understand. This is why I warn against judging any man; you put yourself in position of judging Me and My work! (John 6:44)

Know that I the Lord am watching over you and your family. I hear your prayers and I am making a way. Spend more time in praise and worship. This draws you closer to Me, I am here for you always. Look to Me for strength, for wisdom, and for peace that passes understanding. My peace I give you. Rest in Me always and you shall be lifted up. Show forth My love to all others. People need love, My People have My love to share, and there is an abundance of love that I shower on you. Be lifted up, always looking up seeking the face of Jesus. Be the child of God I have created you to be: strong in the Lord showing forth His grace and goodness.

MY GOAL

By My hand, I will raise up those I choose as they submit knowing who they are in Me! It is this putting down self that allows Me this opportunity to build My close family! My family, the true heavenly one, is My goal, purpose and My requirement! All of My plans are centered on this wonderful family of My forevermore! In slow Spiritual growth I give time for all truth to come forth. It will be budding as a flower opening in pedals of beauty with color and shades brand new each moment of expansion. Oh My children the heights, depths, breadth, and future that I will expand through and for My family! Come see, know, realize, and live with Me!

This is the day that the Lord has made. I will rejoice and be glad in it." You can rejoice every day if you will look to Me, and seek Me with all your heart. My wish for you is joy and peace. Walk each day confident that you are a child of God. Be confident of My presence in your life, Of My love enfolding you. Face every situation boldly knowing that I am with you. I am your strength and your peace, *"I can do all things through Christ who strengthens me,"* Trust in My Word - the Scriptures, for it was given for you, My children.

OUR KINGDOM

When We work together things only go My way, so learn to be more comfortable knowing this. All things then work together for My Good! I bring to My children only the things they should know that help to bring together all Our good! My good becomes Our good when obedience reigns in My Kingdom! I will build your place in Our kingdom as your obedience grows a new you for Our kingdom! The path to the glory I hold out to all My dear ones is the same for each one, for all are on this path in glory to glory. My glory has no end, We are One! See Oneness with Me as ongoing glory. Ongoing glory is a never sameness becoming more and more. I never change, but My children must change from glory to glory.

I give you joy. I give you peace, and I surround you with My love. Go forth this day confident that I am with you. Listen for My voice, still and soft that speaks to your heart. Follow My directions; give out what I have given to you. There is no limit to My love. Be a channel and dispense it freely, *"Freely, freely you have received, freely, freely give."* Be a witness to My love, shower My love on others. Be an open channel for there is no end to My blessings.

Be strong in the Lord; *"The joy of the Lord is your strength."*

ALWAYS SEEKING

Your planned walk is going along now, see that you stay close and grow and grow into all I have for you. Our way goes on and on, as you are open and growing properly! These aren't compliments they are only a report on your ongoing. All My children have their plans to follow, but they only get going on their plan when they willingly do so "On their own." Unless willingness is **always seeking**, the present individual growth stays the same. This putting off growth in the Spirit, while still in the flesh, provides a barrier to Spiritual grow in the future. The longer it takes the more they will find their place as "Least in heaven"! Seek Me now while you are still in the flesh so I can lead and guide you to My highest place for your eternity.

"You are the temple of the Holy Spirit," and you are filled with power and glory through the Holy Spirit! God has given you this gift when you received Jesus as your Lord and Savior. You are to release this power and

these blessings into your life. Be the child of God He created you to be. Fill your life with the love and peace and joy He has bestowed upon you. "Let everything you do be done in love." See others as God's children, seeing the good in them. Let His Word fill your heart and soul. *"Draw nigh to God, and He will draw nigh to you."* Give praise always to your heavenly Father for the blessings He has showered on you!

I DESIRE

The workings of man have always turned from the workings the Father desires man to have. This self in man is strong, but My children seek Me and find Me by My works around them. Thinking, reasonable men always acknowledge the wonders of My works. In these last days there are still men who seek truth. These are the ones I desire. I call men to Me by truth seeking. Yes, it has always been, and will continue to be, men seeking truth are children I desire. When My Bible is searched it should be for the truth buried there that they hunger for. Find truth in the Word and truth will set you free! I seek, l find, and then bless and watch over true truth seekers. My dear ones find in your hearts this hunger for truth and I will help fulfill your desires!

"Draw nigh to God, and He will draw nigh to you." You are not alone. You are not without power, peace, or the love of God. Rest in His presence and feel whole. Let God's love transform you into a new creature. *"My God shall supply all my needs according to His riches in glory, through Jesus Christ."* Be ye restored and renewed by the love of God. As a child of God you are to claim the blessings He has promised you in His Word. Walk upright, filled with confidence that His presence is about you. You are being strengthened, you have the wisdom of God and you have the peace that passes understanding. Thank the Lord for the blessings He has bestowed upon you. You are loved; you are a child of God.

MY WORK

The worlds and heavens that are yet to be shown to and for man are still building and growing. My work is never ending for My children are never ending. Are they not of My hand, head, and heart? Keep always seeking, and I will never disappoint you. We are to grow closer and closer all of the time. As I have said before to you, I dwell in each child not to dictate and control, but to lead guide and protect. The heavens above and the world about can be very dangerous places. Yes, many are the places untouchable and places unreachable, but all of this I will make plain as We grow together! Our lives of forever will truly take forever to fulfill! Such pleasures forevermore, such wonderful events and places I have yet to show and display. Yes, My dear ones you will never be bored or without plans unfulfilled!

I have given to you the Holy Spirit, which is the Spirit of truth. He is also the comforter. He is also to dwell within you forever. Release His power, wisdom, and blessings into your life. He is the third part of the Trinity, holy and righteous and filled with Godly wisdom. He is My gift to you until We are together. I say, *"For all who are led by the Spirit of God are sons of God."* Be led into righteousness into goodness be filled with My love, peace, and joy. These blessings are being held for you in the Holy Spirit. Keep an open channel between your soul and the Holy Spirit. Receive and be blessed!

HIS DESIRES

The work of Our hands goes on and on fulfilling every dream, plan, and event of God's heart for Us. Yes, each child of God He has appointed to a place of joy forevermore. Perfect union brings perfect completion as He has desired. Soon very soon the start of Our individual walk with Him will begin in all of the loving wonder and care which His way desires. Come dear ones grow closer in Spirit with Him as your Father of forever; start this beautiful walk in love, tender and true! Yes, He has already laid streets of gold and made places of residence for all His desire for Us to take place. He knows all you need, care for, and require far better than you do! Your dreams never touch or come close to the reality of His interpretation of what you can think of. Submit as totally as you can now, in the flesh, for all of His best for you to come to full manifestation! You are already committed so release "self" willing, knowingly, and sincerely. Therefore, giving the Father full reign to pursue all in His heart for you!

Jesus is the light there is no darkness in Him. Walk in the light, you are a light in this world of darkness. Let your light shine forth and bring love into the lives of others. You were created to be a light for the Lord. Walk daily in peace and joy knowing that God's love is your covering. *"Arise and shine, for thy light is come, and the Glory of the Lord is risen upon thee.*

KINGDOM OF TRUTH

It has been and is with great pleasure that I bring these words daily for recording. Here is truth from My heart to be made plain and clear. Truth is the only vehicle to have My words to travel on. Seek truth diligently knowing it is My will for all of My children. What else can satisfy? What else will bring real comfort and learning but truth? Satan has made truth into confusion but I bring only truth for My children to grow closer and closer to Me. Nothing but the truth can live forever, and I am calling My family into My truth of all eternity! Come all who love truth and grow in My Kingdom of truth! Love is where all truth resides; I am love. I am the only source of life and I am drawing all My children by truth in love unto My

Self. There is no eternal life outside of My truth. All My lost children live forever, but outside of My kingdom!

"Come unto me all ye that labor and are heavy laden, and I will give you rest." Rest in the Lord and He will renew your strength and bring peace to your soul. *"Thou will keep him in perfect peace, whose mind is stayed on thee."* Constantly be in prayer and praise and He will lift you up. The Lord hears your prayers and He is faithful to answer; remember, *"The effectual fervent prayer of a righteous man availeth much!"* God is love; He is a loving Father watching over His children. His desire is for you to draw closer to Him. *"Draw nigh to God, and He will draw nigh to you."*

TRUE DESIRE

The world is in great confusion, see that My children are not! Only My true children know Truth for I have opened their hearts, where I live in them, to know truth, and that is the truth that sets them free! Never doubt, never fear for then I must back away from that that you hold. I still allow My children their free choice while they are in the flesh.

Clearly that is My testing place for each one! Consider carefully this here said for in it lays your choice, life or death! My true children know Me, without doubt, without hesitancy! Yes, I test carefully because I am seeking an eternity free of all sin, doubt or unbelief. My dear Ones have My worlds of all blessings to live in forever without fear of any kind. This earth is their place of choosing for now; but I will slowly change the earth's task for a work of My true desire!

I will walk daily on the path you have set before me for you Lord are my strength and my redeemer. Thank you Lord for your presence in my life, thank you for the Holy Spirit and the guidance He brings. I thank you Lord for your daily word, the Scriptures that bring forth your promises to your people. I claim these promises for my life. God is love, and His love is spread abroad in His children's lives. All things are possible in the Lord through faith. Release the faith you have been given in the Holy Spirit. Be a channel of faith and love to all. Let your light shine, showing the way, the truth, and the life of Jesus

The unfolding of truth takes many turns and much thought and understanding. Every child of Mine must come to Me for truth's sake. Jesus is truth. A man's steps are useless unless they are walking truth's path for all their pursuits. I set truth's way for only that course provides everlasting safety! I watch closely over all truth seekers for I have called such to be Mine! Set your goals man by truth's standard and failure shall fade away! My protection covers every turn truth may take. Call on truth and I answer! Seek truth's path and I will open your eyes to all, and know all or anything, that will aid your way! Yes, I watch most carefully over true truth seekers! It is My delight when My children seek truth, for then I know I have a child of God forming that I can trust and support, yes lead and guide along their most productive path. Seek truth to know My hand of watchful care!

Lift up your hearts; be encouraged for your Heavenly Father is watching over you. Have a thankful heart and praise The Lord for His goodness. Have the mind of Christ. Think on the blessings in your life and rejoice for your Father is a loving God, know His Word and live by it. Let His righteousness be your righteousness. Live by the Word of God, loving the Lord and others as He has loved you! *"Arise, shine; for thy light is come, and the glory of the Lord is risen upon thee"* God is Love, God is light, and there is no darkness in Him. Replace the darkness in your life with the light of the Lord.

EVERLASTING TRUTH

In these pages, I have released truth for the children of faith to know and realize that truth will never change. I speak truth that is everlasting truth for evermore, for is not Jesus Christ truth? My children must hear truth, see truth, walk in truth and live in truth as I do! Come now dear ones and open your hearts to understand this that I say now, and that I have been saying. The heavens are My truth, the earth is My truth and My children's place of forever is truth. How could all of this that I say not be truth? truth says Mary was the mother of Jesus yet I say in My Word, and here and now, Jesus is My Son! My truth says and shows many things not clear to man in the flesh, yet he is to believe in all that My truth tells! For man to believe in all of the unseen, and unknown, and the incomprehensible he must learn to believe in Me! Yes, I am truth forever, so all truth is of Me!

Walk uprightly being directed by the Holy Spirit. Seek the face of Jesus in all your activities. Live in Him as He lives in you. Let His righteousness channel the love He has for you to all others. Do not store up the blessings He has bestowed on you, but be a source of blessings for others. *"Freely, freely you have received freely, freely give."* Receive and develop the fruit of the Holy Spirit, be at peace, filled with love and let joy fill your heart. Have all the faith and patience with which God has blessed you. Pass it on in love. Let self-control be loosed in your life for it too is a gift from God. Live in gentleness and goodness all the days of your life being meek and good natured. For this is the will of God for your life. All these blessings are available in the Holy Spirit. Praise God!

GROWTH IN TRUTH

I show in these words and pages, truth that I stand behind! It is good for My children to know and understand where My truth lies and what truth means to Me. Each child of Mine should follow truth wherever it leads. Jesus is truth follow Jesus. Here is a simple path that truth follows, a path that the eye can see, the heart can feel, and the ear can hear! My Word, the Holy Bible, is founded on the principal of truth flowing. True words build My children up; Truth is a foundation worthy of carrying all truth holds. How can any task or precept grow to fulfillment unless truth supports it? Seek truth is not only good advice but it brings thought to the question "What else is there" that's worthwhile if it doesn't have its life and growth in truth?

In the fullness of time you will know all things. Now you are to act on the things that you do know. Act according to scriptures, My Word to you. Receive the blessings I have told you about. Have the mind of Christ. Receive and fill your life with the fruit of the Holy Spirit. Live in peace and harmony with all men. *"Let everything you do be done in Love."* My Word to you is; *"And thou shall love the Lord thy God with all thine heart, and with all thy soul and with all thy might."* Also, *"A new commandant I give unto you, that ye love one another, as I have loved you, that ye also love one another.*" Love is the key to all things, everything else will follow.

TRUTH IN YOU

Yes, I say again seek truth forevermore, and then I can open eyes to see Me and Mine. I give hearts to live, know and feel all My truth forever! As for My dear ones, I hold nothing back from them, I give them My image and My likeness that they should always be safe, secure and "My preciseness" alive. Yes, always, in all ways, in every truth I own, for have I not promised? In My words lie all I have past, present, and future. All is clear before Me, and this clearness I will open slowly to all of My children. Stay in truth, love in truth and truth will live in you!

SEE MY HEART

In Our pursuit of truth, always realize truth is all I can use to show My righteousness and My true plans for My children. How foolish is man to assume that I ever endeavor to skirt truth or to show things that are not of truth! All truth is the only path to "believing." If you believe it must be in truth. How can belief survive if truth isn't its foundation? You, My dear ones, can only follow truth, for if that is not so how could you ever belong to Me? Many times you may believe the things I speak of could not be truth, but My children whom I have called, will still carry on by receiving and believing, knowing I am a tester of their faith. Where can faith grow if not surrounded by some truth, or kind of truth? The enemy of your soul survives by lies and untruths that is his only weapon. Yes, I use that to test and examine My dear ones. How else can I bring true hearts to My forever? Dear ones try to see through all deception to find My heart in things. I must try and test all who I draw into eternal life for nothing else will safe-guard all of eternity!

"Thy will be done in me and through me oh Lord, my strength and my redeemer." *"Let this mind be in you which was also in Christ Jesus;"* You should desire to be like Jesus, and to have the mind of Christ, and to see others with love as He sees them. Be ye kind and gentle with a loving heart. Let the Spirit of peace fall upon you and give you rest. My children, see a need and fill it. *"And let us*

not be weary in well doing; for in due season we shall reap, if we faint not." You are led by the Holy Spirit to be true sons of God. Love others as I have loved you!

MY SHIELD

When evil flairs up, I will hold My shield of protection about My loved ones. All My children have their walk through life's difficulties, this too is My testing. Think it not strange when hardships fall upon you. But know who you belong to and rejoice in troubles, for I am with you! I am building My family My way; all My children are My responsibility! Cast your cares upon Me for I love you and watch over you! As your lives unfold know to whom you belong, and rejoice! Testing, trials, tribulations, and separations all these things are worldly that I watch over. Faint not nor fall away for I am with you always. Come My dear ones live not as the world lives but live for Me day by day and I will, Yes, I will, make your way My way!

"He leadeth me in the paths of righteousness for His names sake." Be ye open to the leading of the Lord. In the silence hear His

voice. Know in your inner being what God is leading you to do. Keep your mind fixcd on Jesus, and *"have the mind of Jesus Christ."* The Holy Spirit will show you all things of the Lord. Wait on Him, listen for His soft voice. Know in your heart that you are a child of God and His will is the path for you to follow. *"Thou will show me the path of life: in thy presence is fullness of joy, at thy right hand there are pleasures forevermore*!

SIT UP AND LISTEN

Oh that all My children would still themselves and sit and listen to Me. Then I would open up their understanding, individually, so each one would grow in stature as I desire! But no I must pursue "all ways" to shake and wake each one to draw closer to Me on their own as I can reach them! Those who will be obedient to My written Word I can then reach their ear to teach and draw them into their very own individual task to bless and please Me! My family can only grow into the loving, caring, obedient one I desire by finding their place, each one, by their own obedience to My will and way! This is the most important goal of this work I have given to you. Can you now draw closer, as I desire, with all of the time and attention in these last most important days.

Lift up your head; lift up your heart, for the Father is watching over you. In His infinite love and wisdom He is caring for you. *"Casting all your care on Him, for He careth for you."* Have joy in your life for this is the will of the Father. See all others through the eyes of Jesus. See the good in all the people. See and expose the good in you. All darkness must vanish as the light replaces it. *"God is light, and in Him is no darkness at all."* As a child of God you too should be filled with His light. Let His light shine forth from you as a beacon so that others may know Him.

MY LOVE

Your care for one another should grow more and more as We draw closer in Spirit. This is then My heart and love showing forth through you. I am the help each one needs to obey My command to love one another. That statement never meant for man's love to grow for each other, but it means for My

love to be spread through each child of
Mine. The only way to be obedient to that
command is for each child of Mine to
receive Me in My fullness of love, so that
will release to others until all are family I
care for. The simple truth is not made simple
and easy to obey until a child of Mine is
Mine in all the truth Our oneness can
release. See oneness as your goal and all
these things I demand can be easily released
in your total obedience. My dear ones let go
of self and self-pleasing and all My way can
flow in eager reasonableness!

Rise up, oh ye child of God, rise up and do
the will of God. Trust that you are a part of
God's family here on earth. You have a life
to lead in Him and through Him. He is
always with you; His presence is your
strength, His presence brings you wisdom,
His presence enfolds you and lifts you up to
higher places. Therefore, act accordingly, in
strength and wisdom, always in love, going
forth doing the will of God. *Thy will be
done in me and through me, oh Lord my
strength and my redeemer.*" Be ye
empowered by the Love of God. Step out
boldly, trusting that the Lord will see you
through.

TRUTH'S FLAG

By you reviewing My words to you I can open up truth upon truth. Truth unfolding that I can make a great blessing to all and anyone who will indulge themselves in these words of Ours! Words are carriers of great gifts. But great gifts can come in packages with great wonders and surprises. My gifts can keep on giving when they are given the place of trust, truth, and believing required to acquire them. I can give My dear ones gifts that "keep on giving" when they are unwrapped slowly, thoughtfully, and attended with inquisitive care. All My words can carry depth and ideas requiring probing and digging into with True hearts searching with hope and faith! Total, complete attention to the things here written will bring forth much at first glance, but delving deeper will prove a well of great depth, filled with wealth, and wonder! Just so is My Holy Bible when My true truth seekers will prove this fact to themselves when time is properly applied to their reading efforts. Seek truth and truth's flag will flutter and wave showing worth and wonders to behold!

Study and know My Scriptures so you will know My will for your life. Also claim and receive the blessings promised in My Word. You are a child of God, rise up and do the will of the Father. Let the joy of the Lord permeate your being, let love and peace cover you always. My presence is your strength; it gives freely to others as I have given to you. Be a listener, have a caring heart and pray for those who need help. Let the love of the Lord flow through you and be uplifting to others.

MY REALITY

These days are fast closing and soon the true truth of My reality will flow open as never before and never again! Yes, this that is just before you will have ramifications forevermore! Trust Me, there is just before My dear ones revelation of untold wonders, truth bursting with such a force of beauty that all doubt and unbelief vanishes before your very eyes. Oh, My dear ones stay the course, keep ever seeking more and drawing closer for I am so real and so desiring to prove to you your reality in My forever place of wonders. My children's pictures in their heart and mind can never carry anything coming close to My true reality in Spirit. What a gift is given that so many know not of! Man's imagination flees at My realities presentation! Come dear ones now and draw together in the plan of this that I am now speaking, for this will be in your heavenly interest forevermore!

In the early morning seek My face."*Be still and know that I am God.*" Have the mind of Christ for you are My children. Think not on the worldly things but focus your mind on the things of God and His righteousness. You are not of the world but of My realm in heaven. Come out of the darkness and dwell in the light. "*I am come, a light into the world, that whosoever believeth on Me should not abide in darkness.*" My children, walk in the light. Keep your eyes and thoughts on Jesus and His way. For His way is one of righteousness and love. Draw nigh to God, and He will draw nigh to you."

PURPOSE TO PERFORM

Keep always open to My guidance allowing your closer walk to grow. This is the only course to follow and the only way I lead. Seek always more of My teaching so your life will show My hand upon you. Our walk has all of the Father's purpose to perform. Just stay always aware of who you are in My presence, acting as My word source shown! This is unique not a worldly way, but working as My hand on pages of display. See that your purity grows in proportion as Our closeness grows. This is a big task and you'll need all I can share with you to continue to please the Father. Yes, this is different, but I am the God of differences as all My children slowly will see and know. Our times together have much further to go so let this closeness continue to grow. See My hand of guidance more in what you are doing, and have more confidence in this that is being done! I am not a purposeless God, but only My purpose do I show! When only My will and way is on your daily display will there be time to work and play?

Rise up and worship the Lord, your God. Know that you are the temple of the Holy Spirit. You have been given the Holy Spirit and the fruit therein. Live abundantly by releasing these blessings into your life. *"I have come that they might have life, and they might have it more abundantly."* Live

the abundant life Jesus has made possible
for you. Rise above the worldly things and
into a life with Jesus. He is your strength,
your peace, your joy and wisdom. *"He
which hath begun a good work in you will
perform it until the day of Jesus Christ."*
Persevere for He is your strength. Rest in
Him and be renewed. *"Trust in the Lord
with all your heart, Lean not on your own
understanding."* Let your faith carry you
through all things.

FINAL PURPOSE

Let not Our progress stall, but follow on
drawing closer and closer as the days ahead
come to their final purpose. All time use
comes in sections and blocks, and this
particular Time of the Gentiles is quickly
closing. This has dire consequences for all
left on earth for Israel's closing! Knowing
this that I am speaking about means only
one thing to the children of My purpose, the
ones of My choice. **"Wrap up quickly your
chosen place with Me."** I give this now as
loving advice for all and any who hears and
knows My truth for Him! Yes, these closing
days are open to your choosing time of a
place with Me. Are you clear on this that I

here say, if so this word is your "blessing divine" given at this time. If not ,you will be left with what you already have chosen as your place with Me. A useful loving child or only the least in heaven! Decide where you desire to be with Me, for your time left grows shorter and shorter, fast becoming none, *NO MORE ON EARTH!*

Let the peace of the Lord flood over you. Let His love enfold you, and let the joy of the Lord become your strength. For the Lord God is always with you, His presence abides with you. Let My words be your words, pray and meditate on the scriptures for they are life unto your being. *"For He will give His angels charge concerning you, to guard you in all your ways." "He will call upon Me and I will answer him, I will be with him in trouble. I will rescue him and honor him."* My children know My words to you are true!

FOREVER ONENESS

It is with great joy that I draw all My children unto Me. This is no small thing that is now, and has been in work since, even before, the creation of the heavens and earth. This unfolding of My plan of eternity, where

My heart and joy is ongoing, will forever be before Me and My loved ones. Our oneness grows in daylight and in darkness throughout ages past and ages yet to unfold. This is eternal ongoing unfolding My love in large and small detail! Growth, eternal life forever, no end even imagined and never planned! My children are now joining Us in life eternal to know love expanding. My handiwork is exposing only love's dreams and desires, while bringing My ever increasing family into their forever oneness.

Each one of My children is special to Me and I watch over all of them. God's love is covering the world. There is light, God's light in spite of the darkness in this world. Know Him and His love. Be confident that He is here. You are a child of the living God and He cares for you. He is your refuge and your fortress, a God you can always trust, no evil will befall you, and He will give His angels charge over you. So rest in Him, take of His love and grace and trust in His word to you. *"I will never leave you, nor forsake you, even to the end of time."*

THE WORD BURIED

When My Word is buried in My children's heart then We will walk as One. Jesus is My Word and when Jesus is buried in My children's heart We will walk as One! When I am buried in My children's heart We will walk as One. Only My children will open their hearts and welcome all I have prepared for them. I hold back nothing when their willingness meets My desires. I say they are joint-heirs with Jesus. Yes, I open all to My Son Jesus, and as all My children open their hearts to us they are given all of their inheritance. All I have will become all they have for are We not One? Come behold the great blessings and wonders that I hold before all who turn to Me in total obedience. Are you not made in My image and likeness for such as all this that I speak of? Have I not said, "Ye are Gods?"

"Blessed is the man who perseveres under trial because when he has stood the test, he will receive the crown of life that God has promised to those who love Him." Receive the promises that God has promised you because you love Him. You should be an

open vessel with the love of God flowing in and the love of others flowing out. Stand fast in your love, knowing that He is with you. He is your source of all things, *"But seek ye first the Kingdom of God and His righteousness, and all these things shall be added unto you."* Look to Him in prayer and be in constant prayer for this is your connection to God and His power. Let your prayer be filled with adoration, confession, thanksgiving and supplication, for this is the will of the Father.

HEART NOT HEAD

Draw ever closer all the time now, for that is to your great advantage. Give Me more attention, more time, sit in silence more, allowing My blessings to flow more readily! Do not hesitate when truth is flowing readily! Build now a sturdy foundation solid and true. Yes, do only things that I ask, and soon you will grow more and more. Only My way should prevail, so seek My daily way moment by moment now. Make the worth of listening into a more noticeable blessing daily! Nothing is really accomplished by your "trying harder" only obeying the things I ask counts now! Seek heart obedience not Head obedience! Proper understanding comes when the heart knows and tells the head! But only quiet, still heads can hear. You're more perfect walk follows you heart not your head! My still voice dwells in your heart, Listen!

Stand before your Lord with a clean heart, for your God is a forgiving God. Through His shed blood you have been washed clean, your sins are forgiven, therefore go forward doing the will of God. Love His children as He has loved you. Be patient and understanding in all situations. Let the Word of the Lord come forth from your mouth, always positive, trusting God for all things. *"The joy of the Lord is your strength." "I can do all things through Christ which strengthens me."* With His promises on your lips and in your heart you will be lifted up. You should rest always in the Lord knowing that He is doing a work in and through you. Remember: *"They that wait upon the Lord shall renew their strength."* Go forth trusting, for God is faithful to His Word and He loves you!

THE TRUE PATH

My "Words of Wisdom" I bury not unseen or unheard, yes, from the time of Job I have opened My heart to My listening obedient children. To those whose attention I gain I show favor and blessings. Yes, even in hard and difficult ways is My deep love shown to them. How else is true gold found but through refining? By the time of Job I did allow men to find in the earth My valuables for them, all minerals and worthy metals for their use. I will not hold back wealth from My children, but I will restrain My love until truth is clear and made the badge of worth for them to wear. Yes, the pursuit of My love through truth is the true path for all men to follow. There is no gift more precious or worthy for men to cherish than the gift of My image and likeness. Seek Me in truth pursuing My love and I will pour out all heaven and earth before you!

Call on the Lord for all your needs. Stay in constant communication with Him. Praise and worship Him."*Trust in the Lord with all your heart; lean not on your own understanding. In all your ways acknowledge Him and He shall direct your path.*" Be directed and guided by the Lord. Listen to His directions, know and be guided by the Holy Spirit within. God's best is for you if you will but listen and hear His quiet voice. Have faith and patience knowing that God is working in your life. Trust Him for He cares for you. Receive and live in His love, encompassed by His presence and grace. Special words of faith for this will strengthen you and lift you up.

IN THE AIR

See that We draw closer and closer now for Our walk is worth more and more. Keep always close in My Holy Bible and in My presence. The closing time is upon the earth and the great separation is progressing. Now is the time for all My children to draw closer and closer in preparation for that great event in the air. Why in the air, because it is the closest and cleanest place near you who are still on the earth. Yes, the view of the earth will be quite prominent when We meet in the air. Isn't this most appropriate as a place for Our first wonderful gathering having the beauty of the earth in Our background? This is a one last look for My dear ones before departing to My present heavenly place. Just know with growing confidence all is prepared and on schedule!

Know the will of God! *"Be still and know that I am God."* In the stillness God's presence will be manifested, for He is always with you. Trust that He will lead and guide you through all situations. *"Trust in the Lord with all your heart,"* for He is a faithful God, filled with love and peace. Go forward boldly, child of God, knowing that He is with you in love and peace. Stay connected to the Father through prayer and praise. Have a heart of thanksgiving for He is your source of all things. *"I am come that they may have life, and that they might have it more abundantly."* Believe God's Word to you!

TRINITY SPEAKS

This walk is a most timely one for My calling to be made clear to My dear ones. **Only Spiritual growth I require is important now.** The worthy ones will I personally teach, guide, and talk to now! I must gather a group to hear, listen, obey and do. You must choose the right walk for My heart to prepare your heart for a place of worth to Me! <u>Jesus and I are in this teaching through My Holy Spirit</u>; this is the last perfect method I have chosen to build a worthy true hearted group to be prepared for

My Kingdom work. Yes, this is My most important starting place for fulfilling My future heart's desire. A kingdom must have a faithful ruling house, and Mine is no different. Management support systems have been taught by man, but none like I teach! Each heart gathered has "passed the muster" so to speak. My muster, that is. Keep ever drawing closer dear ones!

Let the Word of the Lord be your strength, your protection, and bring forth wisdom and fill Your life with joy. *"Thy Word is a lamp unto my feet, and a light unto my path."* Rise up child of God; let your light so shine that men would know Jesus through you. The Word tells you, *"Arise, shine for thy light is come, and the glory of the Lord is risen upon thee."* Bring your body and soul into agreement with God's Word for you are now a child of God. Release the blessings He has bestowed upon you. Live in the fruit of the Spirit. Release the blessings within the Spirit. They are yours, a gift from God.

SAY YES LORD

Broad is My reach and perfect is My touch, many I call but few listen, hear, believe and obey. Oh yes many move, but only at their own, timing, and desire. Learn this lesson dear one, **when I call, you answer Me, and then do as I say**! Yes, Our walk is truly the walk I have called you to, not the time, place, or things you decide or desire, but you should only fulfill My desires as I see fit! This is a great time of transition, some never make it in the flesh, some come part way, others only start and try a short while. Be consistent My dear ones and answer My call with all your heart, all of your time, and with all of your love, Then I can draw you "all of the way." Say these words out loud, **"Yes Lord I will listen, hear, and answer, believing and doing!**

Open your ears, open your eyes, and most of all open your heart and receive what I have for you, My children. My blessings for you are endless, waiting for a receptive heart. *"Delight thyself in the Lord and He shall give thee the desires of thine heart,"* My children look to Him, and desire a closer walk with the Lord. *"Draw nigh to God, and He will draw nigh to you." "Be still and know I am God."* In the stillness, with your heart longing for more of God, He will make His presence known. He will impress upon you His will for you, His love for you, and you will know peace!

HEAR, LISTEN, OBEY

As I come to My children now, it is to speak to them believing that some will hear and heed that which is said. It is well for all that will listen, hear, and do! The Bride of Christ is in that position now and so few are obedient. These then are times of great opportunities for obedient children to be taught by Me, for I will willingly tell them their best path to follow. Only those willing ones who listen, hear, and obey can be given the things on My heart for them. Only I know the plans and dreams I have for their future good will. This is Truth disclosed for the readers benefit. Yes, dear ones wake up to the most important things for you to learn and know and do! All I write here is victory, blessings, and gifts from flowing truth! This is My will and way but so few will enter and play!

"I can do all things through Christ who strengthens me." Rise up and take My Scriptures for yourself. Claim them as promises to you for they are, if will trust.

You have a measure of faith through the Holy Spirit within you. Release the faith power and develop it in your life. Keep My words in your soul and Spirit so that you may grow in faith. *"Draw nigh to the Lord and He will draw nigh to you."* Keep always a connection between you and the Father for He is your source of all things. Be connected to His power and receive His grace.

WALK OF ETERNITY

This day is important, as is every day I give you to make you Mine! Not until My children learn this as they learned "Self," will We have that close "walk of eternity" I desire and eagerly wait for! Yes, dear ones I too am waiting for Our glories to come! Keep always, yes even after your translation, this eager anticipation to be "doing Our doing" together! What a time that will be, "Ever ongoing" with a joy and happiness not yet fully conceived and understood by My dear ones! I have plans extending into My realms of wonder and beauty that I cannot say enough in "earth words" for they are inadequate to convey all truth to flesh in meaning ways. This kind expression of Mine must be taken by you as I intend for it to be. Only a blessing little understood, but expanding and extending into your forever with Me!

Our Heavenly Father, God, so mighty and powerful, all seeing, all knowing, and yet He is with each one of His people and knows each one completely. He hears our prayers and answers them. *"The effectual fervent prayer of a righteous man availeth much is his promise to us."* *"And all things whatsoever ye shall ask in prayer, believing, ye shall receive."* He is concerned about each one of His children and hears your prayers and answers them. God is a personal God filled with love. He knows your needs and fills them if you draw nigh to Him. God's love is never ending and everlastingly.

TRUE HEARTS

I have full and complete plans available for any child of Mine who will spend time with Me. It is only in this manner I am able to lead, guide, instruct, teach and truly show I am their Father. How else, or in what better way, could this be done? Yes, I desire to become so real to My dear ones in this manner while they are still in the flesh. It is best that I pick and judge their future position with Me in this time and method. For only then will I be dealing with their true hearts in the flesh time! Later after the rapture their knowledge will be so well informed that their judgment then is influenced by their circumstances. Does this give some better explanation of why **I prefer to find true hearts in the flesh?** These become solid rocks that I can trust and use to build My Kingdom. See now the connection that counts to build your future? This is truth not before revealed! Truth most precious! See that it is used wisely and truthfully!

Let your life be guided and directed by the Holy Spirit. Sit in silence and listen for the Word of God is in your heart. Be aware of His great love for you. He imparts that love and peace from himself unto you His child. Have an open heart and receive all He has for you. Be ye lifted up by His presence. The fruit of the Holy Spirit within you is awaiting your release. To live a more productive life you must increase in love, peace, and joy. You must release the patience, self control, and faith the Holy

Spirit has for you. Always have meekness, gentleness, and goodness as your attitude for this is the will of God for you.

TRUE LEARNING

If the learning for man was to be all self-taught where would that leave Me? No My dear ones true learning means learning My truths that I teach man for only I know each man's true needs and capabilities to absorb that which he must learn to properly grow as My child. True learning means learning My truths. Man's teaching is so infiltrated by Satan thinking that man is eventually contaminated beyond rescue by man, only I can save such a one. I am very jealous of My children and I desire each one to come to Me. Learn to grow closer by meeting Me in the early morning, in the silence, where I can gain full attention. Then in secret I can bring Spiritual knowledge that draws the soul into Spirit thinking. (*Let that mind be in you that was in Christ Jesus.*) Pay more attention My children to *"Revelation Knowledge"* that I can bring than all the studying you can do on your own! We are One only means when you can give up self! Self twists, considers, and thus contaminates truth and true teaching. Only by My Spirit and by My love will My children gain the place I have for them!

"Arise, shine, for thy light is come, and the Glory of the Lord is risen upon thee." Take this Scripture, My Word to you as truth and something already accomplished. For truly My light is upon you. As a child of God you are a light, a beacon showing the way for others who are in the dark. Do not be heavy laden or walking under a heavy burden, but truly rise up. Lift up your head and receive what God has for you. Receive what Jesus Christ made possible for you by His sacrifice. Let your light so shine that others may see Jesus in YOU.

TRUTH WALK

Yes, I have buried much in these daily words that carry life forevermore to any "I lead them to." Be careful about what you share too freely, for only I can support and build in someone the truths I bring. Truths I bring are the key here. Always check with Me when thinking of sharing these truths here given. My true path for all My children is through the growth path of truth exposed.

I do this only when Truth shown is the seed to be gown. Fertile soil is first prepared soil, properly prepared that is. Only I can prepare "heavenly soil" in My children's hearts this is truth sown that must be properly shown! Only eyes open to My truth will ever be blessed with all My blessings as I have purposed. This true truth walk is one carefully planned, planted, watered, and cared for! All takes time applied in learning the progressive steps I've prepared for each child's life with Me.

"Blessed is the man who perseveres under trial." Know that I am with you at all times! You can overcome all things through Jesus Christ who strengthens you. Call on Me, lean on Me, have confidence in My love. Continue to push through the problems and you will come out on the other side victorious. I will not put more upon you, more than you can handle. Be patient in your overcoming. Lessons are being learned, there is Spirit growth. It is so necessary for your closer walk with the Lord. *"Seek ye first the kingdom of God and His righteousness, and all these things shall be added unto you!"* Claim My loving promise to you.

Make it always a joy when We are together, many times My children come to Me heavy and over-laden when they should come to Me sooner, before the hand of the world holds them down. Keep drawing closer all of the time, not just in the early morning only! **When you make the whole day a time with Me** then I can make it your special time of growth. All Spiritual growth happens only when We are drawn closer by your desires for closeness. Only as this desire in you, which is My desire, grows until physical action on your part makes it true will I be released to give freely these things of My heart for you!

I thank you Lord for your ever presence in my life. Help me to be led by the Spirit of God so that I may be a child of God! This is My heart's desire My child, rest in Me, know that I am with you always and My Word promises you, *"He which has begun a good work in you will perform it until the day of Jesus Christ."* God is faithful to His Word. His love is forever an absolute. Live in the light of the Lord, *"God is Light and in him is no darkness at all.*" Cast out all darkness and negative thinking. Fill your being, and your mind, with Jesus and His love. His love is healing; His love is wisdom, *"The joy of the Lord is my strength."* Claim My words for they are promises to you!

OUR TIME

When Our time together seems to drag along what do you imagine might be wrong? Yes, it is true Our time will not always be perfect because you are still in the world and in the flesh. It is this very condition that you should revel and be most happy about, because you are in just the right place at just the right time to be more and more of a blessing to more and more people. Pray for and watch for your opportunities opening to bless My children. Many are there who are "ripe for the picking," and as I guide you draw them closer to Me with the words you will speak. Yes, there is to be two great harvests; one for lost souls, and one the searching hearts. The lost souls are obvious, and the searching souls are My Spirit-filled ones who need further guidance to complete their walk properly with Me. These are where My hopes lie for Our growing times toward the Spirit-filled place I have in My heart for the leaders of Our heavenly kingdom!

Lift up your head and look to your Lord and Savior Jesus for all things. Trust in His love. God has created you to be His children. Have the mind of Christ, and know that you are the temple of Holy Spirit, a part of God given to you. He was imparted to you as a love gift when you accepted Jesus as your Savior. Have a heart full of thanksgiving for the power and promises in the Holy Spirit. Loose these blessing into your life as you draw closer to the Lord. Allow your faith to grow daily as you experience His love and blessings in your life. All things are possible through Christ who strengthens you. *"Thou will keep him in perfect peace, whose mind is stayed on thee."*

GROWING OBEDIENCE

As your days fly by, do not leave My work undone! Pay closer attention to the things I say that you should do! In here lies the blessing of working with Me. Growing obedience brings growing responsibilities and this means a close and closer walk is needed each day now! See My hand more and more on all that I lead you to do. Follow My voice, way, and will to grow as I desire for you. Yes, this means listening more closely, more often and doing new and different things. Wind up these books, and then We can start new and different things to do!

Let the glory of the Lord show the way. Let the mind of Christ be within you for truly you are a child of God, a part of the family of God. Be in tune with the Lord and know His purpose for your life. Walk in this way, His way for you brings peace and joy. Do not strive in worldly matters but, *"But seek ye first the kingdom of God and His righteousness, and all these things shall be added unto you."* Let the Lord direct your path. Maintain a close connection to Him and He will show the way. Rest in the peace of the Lord!

START NOW, DIFFERENTLY

A walk of purpose has an ongoing of forever to seek. Buried in My words are many thoughts to be brought to the surface when sitting in silence seeking! Make more time for this sitting in silence, for this kind of time spent can surface great words or works to inspire! Try seeing into these words I bring the deeper Spiritual side to things of which you are not at presently aware. Only through confident seeking do I release Heavenly word pictures of great worth. Test and try these thoughts I bring for in their release your heart will sing! All learning is not by reading man's written words. Much more of greater worth and depth comes from delving into seeking ideas "I lay before you." To meet Me for greater learning should be your ongoing purpose to pursue, for I will open much of great earthly purpose as well as heavenly help. Eph. 1:3 *"Blessed be the God and Father of Our Lord Jesus Christ, who has blessed us with all Spiritual blessings in heavenly places in Christ:"* Look to Me for all things, I am your provider. *"My God shall supply all my needs according to His riches in Glory through Jesus Christ."* My promises to you are true I am a faithful God. Raise up your faith and know My love. You are a child of God, I am your Father. *"I wish above all things that thou mayest prosper and be in good health, even as thy soul prospers."* Rest in Me, have

faith in My promises to you. Allow My love
to work in your being, be in peace, and the
joy of the Lord will be your strength.

THE TREASURE

In all that I have had you read nothing is
more important than My notes that *I Love
You*! Keep this always foremost in your
heart and mind. In this is the treasure of Our
walk together in fruitfulness, happiness,
love, and peace, forever and forever right on
through *ALWAYS*! No child is without this
tie to My heart! Many are hard to catch and
hard to hold, but I do this for Love's sake! I
love them all, each one that is the only
strong tie of forever. Their love only grows
as time, and hearts find more and more of
Me. I am endless and My newness never
stops. It is in this discovery that children of
worth can be brought forth and identified.
Few children ever climb very high on their
own. If their heart is willing then I can draw
them higher and higher into My planned
place for them. I desire steady, slow
growing, loving attention from each one as
Our path increases in worth more and more.
Always keep seeking in Spirit and then
things of great worth will surround you!

When the fruitless works of man hold him close I am left just waiting. These things should not be! I seek those who seek fruitful works that My hand can guide My dear ones into! Seek My voice, hear My words for you, then I can guide your path into heavenly places! Yes, dear ones listen to truth for only by My words "just for you" will you find My completeness that you should be seeking. Make of great importance this that is here written for these words **are your key that opens My heart more and more.** By these things that I say, you may be lifted up into the place where all your paths are gold and all your dreams unfold! Dream not My dear ones when realities door has swung wide open beckoning! Read My truth. Let it ring in your heart of hearts so as to shake and wake you into all belief I freely give. Time is to your detriment now, be not slow to respond for then your times of regrets will be extended! Open your heart to truth, and truth, this that is here written, will open the true windows and doors of My desires for you!

"Blessed is the man who perseveres under trial." Go forward knowing that I am with you. Trust in My promises to you, have the mind of Christ and keep your mind on Jesus your Lord. He will see you through. *"Trust in the Lord with all your heart."* For He is faithful, He is ever present and His love endures forever. *"For our light affliction which is but for a moment, works for us a far more exceeding and eternal weight of glory."* God's plan for us is filled with love, and if we faint not our reward in Heaven is forever glorious. Receive His love and His strength, His joy and peace, and you will have the abundant life He has promised.

THE WILL AND WAY

Truly the doors of heaven can and will open when My true ones open up into the will and way I put before them. It is this putting before them that seems to put a wall up. A barrier of self that fools them into thinking this is their last protection. It is this lie of Satan that so easily misguides when only My voice in their heart is what they should be paying attention to. Let this truth that I bring be the loudest attraction that you know! Yes, hold all else at bay until you have truly heard all that I have to say. My words to My children are life savers of great worth; do not make them into confetti of worthlessness! However, watch over, understand and make worthwhile all this I put before you now, for these truths shown over and over again in different words and ways can become stepping stones to heaven's doors.

ALWAYS TRUTH

What is best for man, to fill their heads and hearts with truth or to flatter and mislead them? Truth, always truth, truth only truth. I am truth's door all who listen learn of Me. I am truth, one hope forever, I will never fail! I am not reluctant but I am careful! Why would I bother with all this that you now see about you if it was all I could provide? I have possibilities far beyond any description I could put into words! But I am not just talk, look into the heavens, and search deep into the sea (of salt water and or of humanity). I have always more and more for you My dear children to find. It is the wise ones who search Me out, for these dear ones I can teach and draw into My truths I desire. The true heart searching will only find satisfaction in truth unfolding! Seek truth forevermore!

"Thy will be done in me and through me oh Lord my strength and my redeemer." Walk each day with the Lord, leaning on Him and being renewed and restored in your body and soul by His Love. Look to what you can do for others, be patient and kind. You are to show forth the Love of the Lord at all times. The Holy Spirit will guide the way if you will release His power in your life. God's love flows to you, send it out and bless others. God's will is to love God and to love others. See Jesus in others, look for the good, magnify what is good, and diminish the evil. Where there is light, darkness must flee. God is light. See everyone through the light of Jesus.

OUR ONENESS

In working with My other children I find I must walk a walk of care and caution. Hearts can be tender and cautious, even to their own hurt. As We seek to draw others into a better place, We must be sure the "tender ones" don't fall through the cracks. Loving care is the oil that must flow always for My words to float upon. Keep this approach in mind more as We carry these words of Ours forward! Give no thought or receive no guilt, with this that I'm telling you it is the way and desire of Mine for all those who do My will. I am opening more and more to you and I must keep you closer and closer to My way and walk! Keep always in mind where We are going together, knowing I'm trying to bring all My children on this kind of path. All are different, all are precious and all must come to Our oneness!

"If ye continue in my word, then are you my disciples indeed, and ye shall know the truth, and the truth shall make you free." To be in the Word is to gain Godly wisdom, to learn to live in peace, is to understand God's will for His family. Let the Word be your foundation. *"He sent His Word and healed them, and delivered them from their destruction."* His Word is your protection and your well being. Stand on the Word, keep it in your heart and meditate on it day and night! *"Thy word is a lamp unto my feet, and a light unto my path."* My children walk in the way of My Word and blessings shall be upon you!

When I lead a child of Mine I must have one who is willing to be lead. I do not force, coerce or demand in any way, this makes a very slow and difficult method of training. How blessed are and will be My children who just knowing see and do! This is the search of My heart to find dear ones open, willing, eager and ready for all or anything I ask. The seeking, searching, and peeking, and looking ones are so much a great a delight to Me. freely give, freely desire, freely be led are those I can inspire. Listening, hearing, understanding and doing are rafts of life I can heap My desires and blessings on; but mainly it's My purposes that I hold dearly. If dear ones would try to get on My island I could show all of them a much better walk in the flesh, and suit them up for much greater positions in Our kingdom!

Live your life as a true child of God. Set your eyes on the heavenly kingdom and rise above worldly situations, trusting in the Lord to show the way. Go forward boldly, keeping your eyes on Jesus. Have faith in the Word, *"But seek ye first the kingdom of*

God, and His righteousness, and all these things shall be added unto you." Let the love of God be your guiding light. Just know, "*But my God shall supply all my needs according to His riches in glory by Christ Jesus.*" You have been given a measure of faith through the Holy Spirit. Release and grow this faith. Know that God in His infinite love will lift you up and make a way. Receive and live in His love!

SEEK MORE AND MORE

It is from the daily attention that I receive from My dear ones that I can tell how fast My children are growing and just where they are going. I watch carefully day by day knowing that where they seek to go I can guide and direct them when We are walking hand in hand, so to speak. However how many are truly following any path I have set for them? Or how many are close enough to Me daily so I can speak and direct their way? These are the very last days of flesh walk for all of My born again ones and so few are able to hear My individual instructions. This is so sad! Seek, search out, find ways to stir and awaken listeners that I can draw close to Me now. Only in this flesh time can I give special helps for them to be taught or shown or told. Seek more and more to draw listeners to this truth told! Yes, kept seeking to teach them to learn to listen to Me in the morning!

Glory, glory, glory! Let the glory of God surround and engulf you so that you may be an effective child of God. Rise above the problems and confusion of the world. *"But seek ye first the kingdom of God and His righteousness and all these things shall be added unto you."* Have God's Word on your lips and in your heart at all times. Let your faith expand as you trust in the Lord for all things. He is a faithful God and His promises are true. Remember His Word: *"Delight thyself in the Lord and He shall give thee the desires to thine heart,"* Desire God's best and expect His blessings in your life.

DRAWING CLOSER

In all the things I've brought before you one thing should continue to be emphasized, **"Always keep drawing closer."** You will do this only one way, "Give Me more time." Never neglect Our morning time, but now it must overflow into the day, hour by hour, until it becomes minute by minute! ***Oneness is Our goal and time is the watch-master***! This today is another step to not be overlooked. Of all of the words I bring, these are the most precious ones, "Come to Me more and more so will Our walk grow into the path of all of Our desire." Your desires will never flourish to the extent that "Our desires" can expand! Just push on and then you'll see the endlessness of more and more! I am showing you this endless climb into My place, The place I desire to draw each and everyone who willingly is drawn into the growth walk of forever! Yes, there are many pausing places, getting off places, and staying off places, as well as ongoing places, each child of Mine has their freedom of choice. Today I am teaching this walk of My wonders so many will see the many ways I will open for My dear ones to grow!

"Thy Word is a lamp unto my feet, and a light unto my path." Go forward in peace and strength for I am with you always. Know that all things necessary for your life I have provided. Learn to receive, and to release these blessings in your life. Look to Me for all things. *"I am come, a light into*

the world, that whosoever believeth on me should not abide in darkness." Walk in this light for you are a child of the Living God. Choose a life with Christ in the light. Live in abundance for Jesus came that you may have life abundantly!

MY WORDS

It is through morning by morning contact that I can keep My words building in your heart in meaningful ways. Yes, there are many ways I can draw My children closer and closer to Me. If that were not so I would miss most children altogether! There is no one set plan that I can use to capture every soul I desire. All this is also a part of My challenge. It is the fact that all are unique that makes this gathering of My family so intriguing. It is through the little differences in each child that I can display the vastness of all that I am! Mankind is truly a display of Me unfolded and unfolding day by day through always! Why do I say We are all One? Have I not said, "Ye are Gods?" Just to explain this statement will take eons of time. My dear ones stay with Me for there is no short simple explanation of who you are in Me! I John 3:2; I Cor. 15:49; John 10:34; Ps. 82:6

Be lifted up by the love of God. Seek His face, have the mind of Christ, and desire to be one with the Lord. Love one another as Christ has loved you. God is truly your source of all things, so put yourself in His holy and loving hands. Release self to Him in confidence that He will provide all things necessary for your well being as well as the desires of your heart. Delight thyself in the Lord and He shall give thee the desires of thine heart! *"Cast all your cares upon Him, for He careth for you,"* Empty self of all negative thoughts and feelings, and let Him fill your soul with love, peace, and joy. The joy of the Lord is your strength so go forward in strength and joy. Be lifted up into the heavenly realm.

GOOD WORK

The hearing of My word that I speak to an individual child of Mine *is a most blessed activity for any child of Mine to engage in. This is the first and real door to My heart.* There are few who will take this path and carry it along daily as I desire, but those who do faithfully listen and give heed to what I say they have already stepped into a worthwhile place in My heart. Keep this work ever on-going *for it pleases Me* and I encourage such activity continue more and more!

My child, receive today what I have for you. Be an open vessel always looking for and receiving My thoughts and My love for you. Grow in knowledge and wisdom through the Holy Spirit. Grow in faith through the Scriptures. *"So then faith cometh by hearing and hearing by the word of God."* Put the Word of God in your heart and let it change your life! Know and hear by God's Word, keep it in your heart and on your tongue. See and hear God's promises to you constantly! Know, *"That He which hath begun a good work in you will perform it until the day of Jesus Christ."*

My child, receive today what I have for you. Be an open vessel, always looking for and receiving My thoughts and My love for you. Grow in knowledge and wisdom through the Holy Spirit. Grow in faith through the Scriptures. *"So then faith cometh by hearing and hearing by the word of God."* Put the Word of God into your heart and let it change your life. Know and live by God's Word, keep it in your heart and on your tongue. See and hear God's promises to you constantly. Know that *"He which hath begun a good work in you will perform it until the day of Jesus Christ."*

CONSIDER CAREFULLY

The victories that I hold out before man can become their everlasting road to My heart only when they become ongoing believers, achieving from all I say to them! To let My words fall on dull unbelieving hearts is a sure path for missing My great blessings! I'm not talking about the unborn again or lost ones, but I am directly speaking to My children who know Me! Growing closer day by day in obedience to what "I say to them" is the only path to My finest and best places. To be saved is one thing, to truly know Me and My heaven's ahead takes a whole different way to walk that few are willing to strive for and achieve. I am here warning of the on-going climb it takes to be where I seek to draw each one I love! Consider carefully this here said today and make it a constant ongoing challenge to all who will listen!

> *Truth is so simple and clear,*
> *yet so difficult to achieve.*

Discipline your life to include more time with the Lord. Listen for His soft voice, have the knowing when He is making His will known. *"Be still and know that I am God."* Desire a closer walk with Him. *"Let this mind be in you that was in Christ Jesus."* My Scripture, My Word, "make it known that these things are possible, so walk in obedience to My will." Remember: *"The effectual fervent prayer of a righteous man available much."* He will come along side of you and help you in all things. Trust in the Heavenly Father. Call on Him constantly, for He hears your prayers and is faithful to answer.

SAVING PRAYER

When the day of the Lord falls upon the earth surely all of My loved ones will have departed, and I will see them, and they shall see Me as I am! So dear ones know truth and truth will set you free in the short time that lies ahead just for you. Many will see and not know or understand the affairs of that day, but My children will know. Make saving prayers a daily practice this will keep Us close and clear understanding will support all who are Mine. Fail not to gather yourselves together more and more as this wind-up carries on about you. Keep ever drawing closer as I desire you to do!

A new day have I given to you, so fill it with peace, with love and with joy, rest in me, *"For my yoke is easy and my burden is light."* Fill your mind with peace, My peace, and you will know My will for you. You will walk in the path that I have set before you. As you go forth, *"Let everything you do be done in love,"* for truly this is My will for you. Your strength comes as you, *"Draw nigh to God and He will draw nigh to you."*

LOVE FOREVER

It is true in all of the works and writings of man, that man has attempted, none can compare with My Bible! I have allowed enough truth to tell man the story he needs to find Me. But it is after men have found Me that they flounder so! It is with following the words of truth I clearly state that men may know more and more of My ways, plans, and purposes. This knowledge, "by Spiritual revelation" is how I will lead those who find this true path to follow. Listen My dear ones and I will speak, bringing truth and guidance, drawing all

men into their planned place of true purpose
I have set for them.

The mind of man will follow either the
Spirit of man or the Holy Spirit I put in their
heart at their new birth! It is this obedience
to which Spirit man follows that determines
man's place with Me. Isn't this clear
enough? My dear ones follow My Spirit
indwelling you so will We walk the eternal
path of love forever!

There is peace in the heart of those who
walk in the way of the Lord. Rest in Him,
and receive His love which produces joy
forever. Always have this wonderful
connection With the Father through Jesus
Christ which sustains you. Let prayer be a
large part of your life. Also put Holy
Scripture, God's Word, in your mind and on
your heart for they will lift you up. There is
power in the Word of God. *"Let everything
you do be done in Love."* Walk the path He
has provided for you and you will be
covered with protection and Love for you
truly are a child of God!

MY SELF EXPANDED

The ruling and reigning of Israel is My main purpose for Israel. They are to forever give forth the children to inhabit My universe. My dreams are far above the dreams of man, for My dreams are for the dreams of man. Man will no more be "Man," but man will forever be "My Self expanded," as all My children will forever be with Me, and I will be in them! We will truly become One as My Holy Bible has indicated. Dreams are for man now, but reality is Our forever together. It is a reality far above anything ever conceived in the heart of man. Truly you are My children now, yet with little understanding of the far reaching truth of that reality. Yes, My Holy Bible holds forth some of these pictures bringing some reality to your hopes and dreams, but **"My dear ones never will Our talks now bring the fullness of Our forever wonders in the making!"**

Show me thy will Father. Make clear the path You have prepared for me, for my heart's desire is to be in Your will. *"For God has not given us the Spirit of fear, but of power and of love and of a sound mind."*

Thank you Father I receive your power, your love and a sound mind. Use the blessings that He has bestowed upon you, show forth His love, believe and walk in the power of the Lord for it is upon you. Know that you have a sound mind. My child walk with Me always, *"Draw nigh to God and He will draw to you."* Walk in confidence that I am with you; let My love be your love and, *"Let everything you do be done in love."*

TRUE PURPOSE

As I have said before, "This walk that We are having together is unique, not as any other." Therefore, it requires more careful attention to what I say to you because it affects many who will read the work We are doing. Words are My vehicle of great worth for by them I will raise up nations and by them I will tear down unworthy works. This that We are doing has more potential than you seem to assign it, do not foolishly miss the point of what We are doing. I only desire to wake all up who are reading this to the great potential of this that We do! Keep My object always in mind as We do this recording of My words daily! What then is My true purpose?

*"To stand truth before My children
as the pinnacle and monument
of Almighty God. Jesus
is truth forever and always".*

*"The joy of the Lord is my strength." "Be
still and know that I am God."* I am the God
that healeth thee, so rest in Me, trust in Me.
Know and live in My love. *"My peace I give
you, not as the world giveth give I to you."*
Have peace and rest in Me and the
restoration will come for you are a child of
God."*Trust in the Lord with all your heart,
and lean not on your own understanding. In
all your ways acknowledge Him and He
shall direct your path." "Surely goodness
and mercy shall follow you all the days of
your life and you shall dwell in the house of
the Lord forever."*

PROPHECY

The affairs of this nation are still in My
hands, and I will work the work of
requirement for these times. I bring ends of
time, and I bring new beginnings as I see fit.
My children, who I know, and who know
Me, are always safe in My hands, but the

wandering disobedient ones will know My hand upon them whether they know Me or not! Yes, I say one time ends and another time begin. "Woe, to those who know me not!"

Your body is the temple of the Holy Spirit. Treat it accordingly, in love and honor and purity. Do not pollute this house that God dwells in. Join together in Spirit and be as One in the Lord. Take unto yourself the holiness of God, His righteousness and His love, be an ambassador for Christ in your daily walk. Let His perfect love shine through you so that others may know Jesus and His love. Walk uprightly, always confident that He is with you, providing strength and peace as well as the love of the Lord. Receive and share all that God has for you, for this is His will for you.

PRAY IT

Our walk has just begun, as you wake up to all this truth that I set before you. **Yes, pray this truth for your life and I will make it so!** All that I say to you, "pray it to make this truth alive in your life for evermore." I open up few children to as much as you have recorded. Learn to use it wisely and I can build Our kingdom upon these things here written. **Yes, pray My words to you as I touch your heart with these eternal truths, and eternal truth will I free for those around you!**

Beautiful truths, wonderful truths, and truths to build a kingdom on.

PRAY THESE TRUTHS

I would have you live your life according to My Word. Seal My words in your heart and make them your guiding light and live by them. *"Let everything you do be done in love."* Have the mind that was in Christ Jesus. *"Draw nigh to God and He will draw nigh to you."* Live in an attitude of love, peace to all, and joy, having a thankful heart. For when you are walking with God this is joy forevermore. Have a thankful heart with praise on your lips for God's goodness and blessings in your life. All things come from the Father, He is your source. Recognize Him as your loving Father, He Who bestows blessings filled with love.

Errors of the children are works of man. Yes, all of Our works come through and are tied into the work results of others output. This is My common experience with even the best of My people. My children will find ready acceptance the best way to handle the errors of the children. Use each lesson I bring before you to help grow your control over your own output for Me. All the children try their best, which falls far short of My best! My best is attainable only when My children are fully Mine! Keep your eyes open daily to more and more lessons and let them make you better, for all truth will come out in time! The morning times are truly your most effective learning times, but you haven't put much attention on these times. Now will be a breakthrough, so receive and continue to walk as I lead you.

Let love cover all things for only through love can God's purpose be fulfilled. Knowledge without love is useless. Bathe every situation in love and prayer so that God's wisdom can come through to you. Maintain an attitude of joy for "*A merry heart doeth good like a medicine: but a broken Spirit drieth the bones.*" Have an attitude or a Spirit of love, peace and joy. *"Create in me a clean heart, oh God; and renew a right Spirit within me,"* Watch the words of your mouth such as negative thoughts, critical attitude, condemnation of others all must go! *"Finally brethren, whatsoever things are true, whatsoever things are honest, whatsoever things are just, whatsoever things pure, whatsoever things are lovely, whatsoever things are of good report, if there be any virtue, and if there be praise, think on these things."* This is the attitude God would have you live in when your mind is stayed on Him!

OUR WALK UNFOLDING

Learn to let Our walk just unfold as you go along each day drawing closer and closer to Me! We have a plan and a path to follow, just allow Me to lead and guide. I will make this time just before you unfold in slow waves of blessings for you and those around you. Draw each one closer as you become more and more aware of whom they are that I am gathering into Our will and way. Keep on your search for My words in the Bible for from them We will build a picture I am unfolding day by day. Yes, Our plan is unfolding and We are truly walking in it together! More time, closer time, all of the time, this is your only path of victory now. Listen, hear, learn, and then teach, bringing all My heavens into reach! Nothing I bring comes without time to let it unfold in its perfection. Just keep in mind, I know what We are doing, Let My peace be your pillow of comfort daily!

Rise up and enjoy the day and the blessings the Lord has for you. Have a heart of thanksgiving. Look around you and see what you can do for others. Be a giver, be a lover of people. Rise above the problems of the world and dwell in My kingdom. I will lift you up if you will look to Me. Have the mind of Christ, and think on things that are positive, lovely, kind, and pure for this is the desire of the Lord. Watch the words of your mouth for they are powerful, *"Let the words of my mouth and the meditations of my heart, be acceptable in thy sight, oh Lord my strength and my redeemer."*

WORD TREASURE

The treasure of My words is not found in the study of My words, but it is in "the revelation" of My heart that is in the words brought forth. My dear ones I am Spirit and you are growing in Spirit. Your growth depends mainly in "Spirit growth," this is why by "revelation knowledge" only is great growth accomplished! I reach My worthy ones by "revelation knowledge," do you see why? Revelation bursts forth from the Holy Spirit with revelation enlightening your Spirit heart with perfect insight into My subjects of worth, then your Spirit heart teaches you soul (mind) with useful understanding. This is the way for all of My children to draw closer to Me day-by-day! This is how the Father desires to bring each child of His into His personal way for each one to grow! *THIS IS THE WHY OF JOHN 6:45!*

"Thy will *be done on earth as it is in heaven."* My desire for My children is for each one to kill self in order that the Holy Spirit, the Jesus part, may rise up in you. Make way for the Lord in your life by putting down self. Self is a stumbling block.

Jesus did only what the Father told Him to do. Let us likewise live in this manner. Come against selfish desires, not forgiving, worry and unbelief, by *"Casting your cares on Him for He cares for you." "My God shall supply all your needs, according to His riches in glory, through Christ Jesus."*

TASK MOST IMPORTANT

As you grow you will see that no walk of purpose goes or grows when walked alone. It is this Truth that should stir and awaken anyone that thinks that they have a call from Me. No one walks alone, but many are there that try! Only together with Me will success be achieved! Now it is with this "with Me" that clarity must birth forth! Until there is US there is no place just for you! All time ahead is useful only when your walk is hand in hand with Me! *This is the task MOST important*, until this is well on its way things will just continue in limbo! Our close walk has been called for and mentioned many times, now is the time for more positive action! The "how" of "this" has been said over and over again so you will understand what's needed!

"Cast your cares on me, for I careth for you." Put your trust in the Lord, and let Him show the way. You have been redeemed from the curse so walk in the freedom that is yours. Put God in charge of all things. Accept everything Jesus' sacrifice provided. Walk uprightly knowing Jesus has made all things possible. Go forth in love and peace with an open mind that can hear from God and solve your earthly problems. *"Thy will be done, in me and through me, oh Lord my strength and my redeemer."*

PLAN PERFECT

As you can see Our work is piling up on Us. Do not be discouraged all is on time. Yes, there is so much to do and so little time, but I am the time maker! These outpourings of My words seems endless, and so they are, but never unplanned. Keep on with the daily reading for that is most required! I am setting the stage as I desire and My plans never fail! Keep always drawing closer and closer for this is a main task for right now. The "how" of all I am setting down on these pages is My task not yours. Keep this reading on going and I will keep the perfect end in sight, only confidence and obedience will prove the worth of these many words. Give your attention more closely to the now that I will show you at the right time and place. Yes, all of this fits into My over-all plan perfect! As brick-by-brick great buildings are created by man, so I with dream upon dream build My wonders to be hold!

"Be still and know that I am God." "Let this mind be in you which was also in Christ Jesus." Let peace, God's peace, flood your soul, through this attitude God can direct your thinking and bring you Godly wisdom. Do not rely on man's wisdom but *"Seek ye first the kingdom of God and His righteousness and all these things shall be added unto you."* Answers to your problems are available if you will but wait upon the Lord, and listen for His solution and His Godly wisdom. Let love be your covering for God is love and He moves in peace and love. "Wait upon the Lord." Trust in Him in all things.

SETTING THE STAGE

These words that I bring to you day by day are truly setting the stage and building to a climax this time on earth for My dear ones. My truth must come before My children now to wake up all who will draw themselves out of the flesh trap into a Spirit walk with Me. My whole plan for man has always been this same goal for all who I call! Many are called but few are chosen, chosen for what? My dear ones you should know this answer in your heart. I never keep vital truths hidden. From the start to the finish, physical birth to Spiritual birth, I have always desired for all My children to grow into the perfection of My Son. This should also be the desire in each ones heart! But sin, sickness, self, and Satan, sets such barriers, that I allow filtering those who walk this path. Can't you see this great necessity I have for the perfection of each dear soul? Some are saved, some are lost, but for those precious ones who walk this trail successfully how truly dear and precious they are to Us!

"He which hath begun a good work in you will perform it until the day of Jesus Christ." Trust in the word of the God. He is doing a good work in you. Lean on Him for He is making a way for you. Have a thankful heart, believing, knowing God's Word is

guidance and promises for you. *"Thy word is a lamp unto my feet, and a light unto my path."* Take joy in the life you have been given. Have always an attitude of peace and love, for this is your gift from the Holy Spirit. See others through the eyes of Jesus, in love and understanding. Through a right attitude and purpose you are growing Spiritually.

RAPTURE

If all the words My children have written about Me were brought together the sky would be filled! Yet nothing past written or nothing still to be written will ever cover the exaggerate beauty of My truth when I fill the air with My beautiful family that I gather from heaven and earth! Such a sight to behold, such a heavenly wonder will fill the air. Myriads of angels, countless members of My family in beautiful raiment all aglow with heavenly light of My blessings. Why in the air? No place is worthy, no place is as grand as My display of beauty that shines as does My family!

No one on earth will see, know, or realize what We are about. Only My angels and My family with no other attraction of any kind, only the goal of all My love in place at one time! This dear ones is My dream to behold, and I hold it before you now so you will make it Your dream! Let the desires of My heart be your greatest desire before you! For truly, We are so close to it you can feel the presence of it now!

Believe the words I have given you. Have faith that you are growing Spiritually. Release more of the Holy Spirit and His teachings and helps to continue growing. My love is your covering and, *"The joy of the Lord is you strength."* Rest in Me for I can bring all things necessary if you will but put down self and let Jesus rise up in you. Believe your God is a God of love and He can make all things possible if you have faith!

TRUE HEARTS

These things that I write to you are for all who will listen with true hearts. It is to the heart of man that I write these things, so they may be more and better informed for these times. I know few believe, but when I find the ones who do I rejoice for then I can gather true hearts for My true works of everlasting worth. Yes, I must have only those who truly hear in their hearts the things of My heart. I do not just randomly seek but I purposely pursue these dear ones who I can trust, use, and bless. No work for Me is lost or useless, but what I choose is forever worthwhile and an everlasting blessing will be forthcoming! You should keep drawing closer and closer as I give you My words to read! Do not diminish or dismiss the worth of truth laid before you! I say it's worthwhile and that should be adequate for all who believe!

OUR WALK

The review of Our walk brings many things more in focus. Looking back exposes errors, lack, omissions, and brings understanding. All is to be of great benefit if properly used! Do not assume it shows lack of success. I am the only One who judges that for you never see into hearts of My children to know what We have done together in their lives! Keep always up and positive as I have been showing you in the mornings. This walk We are on is just a walk! We are not running anywhere! My work is in Spirit and I know what I know! Keep always open, listening and desiring more and more, this is the path I will fill with joy and happiness, seeking always brings My good out! Keep seeking and obeying!

Lift your head, look to Me and be restored, for *"The joy of the Lord is your strength."* Daily rest in Me, and look to Me for directions in all things. Know and believe My Scriptures, *"My God shall supply all your needs, according to His riches in glory through Jesus Christ."* Have peace in your heart knowing that God is watching over you. *"My peace I give unto you, not as the world gives, give I unto you. Let not your heart be troubled, neither let it be afraid."* *"Be still and know that I am God."* I am a loving God. Look to Me in all things and remember, *"He which hath begun a good work in you will perform it until the day of Jesus Christ."* Believe the Word and have faith in a loving God.

MY DESIRE

Yes, I am always with you, and with all My children. Of course My desire is they all may be with Me in body, Spirit, and soul!

How I long for this earth walk to be over and My dear ones all gathered with Me. However, I am also bound to My plan to see all of My loved ones moved through this walk of creation set before them. My dear ones learn to listen, hear, and believe in your hearts for everything I have said, and what I have to say, and to do for you. Time I have given to this gathering from earth to heaven. All things I have set out are to be walked through by all of Us! When I call a family I am obligated just as those I call. Our walk must cultivate in Oneness for all I have planned. Why am I pointing this out now, because a family is only as good as the truth that has brought it together? The truth is everyone, yes, God the Father, God the Son, and God the Holy Spirit; has been and will be as devoted to you as you are. Family is a Oneness of Me and family is and must be Godly!

RESPONSIBILITY

We must in all things learn to draw closer; how else can We become closer? Learn to bring Me closer more and more, for My care of you and yours are requiring more and more. It is your responsibility to bring these things to My attention by inviting Me into them. All this is the more and more of Our growing together. This Oneness that is to be sought for must be claimed, bought, and paid for! Thank your Lord for making this clear. Yes, all your property and work is a source of gifts and tithes; therefore, I should be asked to help. To learn to draw Me into your daily world is to build this Oneness that is so needed for Our growing together!

Stand firm in your faith. God is a faithful God and *"He which hath begun a good work in you will perform it until the day of Jesus Christ."* Truly, *"You can do all things through Christ who strengthens you."* Lean always on the Lord, on your Father, for He is love and will make a way if you are walking in His will. Pray to be shown His will in every situation.

Let your attitude and motive be in love, love of God and love of others. In this way God can use you for His purpose not yours. Hear and be directed from God. *"Be still and know that I am God."* Be filled with wisdom that comes from God. Wait upon the Lord for all things. *"But they that wait upon the*

Lord shall renew their strength." Be renewed daily through your love of God.

THE SEEKING

As you seek you will be rewarded, as you seek first, in the right places, then as you seek with the right motives. The seeking is only the beginning for the journey is as long as it will take you to absorb truth and then learn to walk in that truth in victory! All victory comes about to My children as their obedience to truth flourishes! Behind every endeavor to be sought are the facts of truth to be discovered. Success in searching will come as knowledge in where to seek, and how to seek, is revealed and believed.

As you can see, the drive to win is the real source of strength for victory! One other thing most important, the reason for much difficulty in finding truth for yourself is you may not be seeking for the truth I have called you too, did you ever realize **you must first be on that path** to find sure victory? Come My dear ones find your true walk with Me!

"Cast your cares upon Jesus for He cares for you." Do what you can in every situation through love. Be kind and considerate to all men. Keep your eyes on Jesus. Do not focus on the things of the world. Let God's righteousness cover your thinking and your actions. The Word instructs you to, *"Do all for the honor and glory of God." "Arise, shine; for thy light is come, and the Glory of the Lord is risen upon thee." Do not let the darkness overcome you." "I am come, a light into the world, that whosoever believeth on me should not abide in darkness."* My child you should walk in the light as He is the light.

RESURRECTION

This that you now see is more truth that I desire to be made clear to My children. Too many children just superficially read, hear, or believe things without questions, when it is the seeking, searching and pursuing of truth that they should desire! All truth makes Me more and more apparent to My children. When the inquiring ones truly search for truth I am well pleased and find pleasure in these revelations as they occur. There still lie many interesting truths that should come to light for they all make My reality present today more and more. Yes, all that I gave revelation to are true. All those who willingly open up to the reality of My truths will further make clear all that transpires of My great day of victory. It is only through true truth seekers that such revelations are brought forth!

My children, do all things as unto the Lord. Walk in peace and patience, let love lead the way. Being critical or negative is from the darkness. Replace it from the light. *"God is light, and in Him is no darkness at all."* Jesus brings His Word to you about this, *"I am come, a light into the world, that whosoever believeth on me should not abide in darkness."* Let His light come into your heart and soul that you may be a witness of the love of Jesus. *"Let everything you do be done in love."* Love wipes away sin, love changes everything. God is love.

THE CALL

This walk of each man I call is not to be taken lightly! There are many lost children that day by day are suffering and lost to Me. This should not be! I call all each and every one given birth; but how few ever come before Me in truth seeking? Few are awakened to this call of Mine because only seeking, listening, and inquiring hearts, seem to have the strength of their own salvation to lift themselves up! I call in each heart *but the love of self and call of the world is louder*. I do not shake awake, nor do I force any to listen to My call in their heart. Why, because I'm drawing only those who *desire, seek, and strive to find truth.*

You say I don't remember all this striving, and seeking, but this is because there is a separation in each person from Spiritual reality and earthly reality. To awaken to the call in Spirit requires the soul seeking to go after this love intangible coming from the human Spirit. I am an intangible desire buried in the heart of each one born that must be acknowledged, and many who hear truth preaching are stirred by hearing My truth in their heart, then their soul, mind, or self, must answer that call in their heart. This is all unconscientiously done in the human Spirit. The first awakening occurs in many different ways and situations. This is why a set way is hard to find. There is a necessity for the constant repetitive call to be made so many are the ways of blocking the true call that touches the heart of the lost man. Be patient, be persistent and be loving, thus many will be awakened to truth's call that I can use. ***"Be still and know that I am God."* Hear His voice, be edified by the thoughts He brings you, it is Godly wisdom needed for your life. Let His will for you be known.**

ONENESS PLAN

Our walk will have many phases all are required for proper Spiritual growth. It is the Spiritual growth part where most men come to a halt. The normal man, so called, only then has the real battle with the soul control over the flesh. This is why so many Christians just born again seem to just stop. Oh, they go to church, give money as they see fit, and call themselves Christians. Oh, I will keep them, but great is their loss, for the way of the Spirit life is lost to them, and I find little worth to continue drawing them closer. Here they are stubborn as a mule. Show them your love always with the hope they will break free and follow their Holy Spirit. **Now the true walk I desire is for all of My dear ones to grow closer to Me all**

of the time. This is so seldom taught, and rarely thoroughly or properly, yet Oneness is the goal for all who I draw to Me. Let's spend some time on this Oneness teaching!

Rest in Me, for I am a God of peace. *"I am come, a light into the world, that whosoever believeth on me should not abide in darkness."* Do not strive, but rest in the Lord. Live in the abundant life He has made possible. Know that you are a child of God and He is your strength, your peace and your joy. *"Delight thyself in the Lord; and He shall give thee the desires of thine heart."* Rest in the Lord and know, truly believe that He is watching over you. Know and believe the word, *"Arise, shine for thy light is come, and the glory to the Lord is risen upon thee."* See you incased in His glory, truly a child of God!

ULTIMATE GOAL

My message continues to pour forth when I have listening hearts of obedience. This is My inspiration this is My blessing from the listening, hearing, obeying children. How else can My family truly be Mine unless We are close all of the time? **Believe Me I will**

be as close to all who listen as I will ever be with them in heaven, the place they long for. How else is love shown except by loving presence and communication? *Yes, We will and can communicate now as We will do in eternity!* What does communication indicate? Love flowing should be your answer. *This Oneness I have spoken of is the indwelling presence I desire all of the time.* Yes, start now and it can only grow greater and greater! Learn Oneness on earth and you will have a running start in your heavenly walk of forever! Yes, this is where I'm taking you, and this should be your ultimate goal as it is My ultimate purpose for Us!

NEVER STOP

This writing is saying more and more, I will never stop! My children need so much yet to much and they run away. They are like trying to hold mercury in your hand. Nevertheless, I am always ready, My trying will never stop! What a blessing it is when My children never stop! Stop, where is stop? Where are they who stop? Why stop? I am always, everywhere, all of the time! You too can have this ongoing with Me. ongoing is never stopping, quitting, never turning aside from Me or My plan for you. I cannot open up pleasures forevermore to anyone who is not like Me! For love's sake, for safety's sake, for reasons beyond measures sake. I could give you explanations on and on, but just take My Word now, today pleasures forevermore do not speak of physical pleasures as you now know. My Spiritual life in pleasures is so far beyond anything now known in the physical!

Seek the face of Jesus. Know His will for your life. Rise up above the worldly situations and strife and into His realm of place and purpose, God's purpose. *"Let everything you do be done in Love."* Let your attitude and purpose in all actions be covered in God's love. Commit all things to the Lord. Scripture says, *"Commit thy works unto the Lord, and thy thoughts shall be established."* Have complete faith in the Lord for He is a loving God. *"Cast your cares on the Lord for He cares for you."* Trust that He will perform His Word, *"Thou will show me the path of life: in thy presence is fullness of joy: at thy right hand are pleasures forevermore.*

In Our work time seems to push, but I do not push or drive My dear ones. I only seek to draw them with My loving care and kindness. I try to move them by My desire growing in their hearts. This is why some are confused, there are no hard direct orders given. The drawing through love is time consuming and sometimes My loving way is driven by time and or circumstances. Yes, action is a factor in many decisions, but with love always. My principals are most difficult when working in the physical environment and sometimes misread by unbelievers. My children must know all of the circumstances only bring occasions for them to grow properly. Drawing closer all the time now is your most important path to follow. Learn to listen properly and seek only My way for you all of the time now!

A new day, a new beginning, a fresh start. My child, receive today what I have for you. Be an open vessel, hearing the voice of God, taking in the blessings that are yours. Open the ears of your heart and let Me lift your up. I say to you, *"Arise, shine; for your light is come, and the glory of the Lord is risen upon thee."* Take My promises into your heart and let your faith grow. Do not strive to do My will but rest in the Lord, confident that He is doing a work in you. You will be strengthened through the power of God. *"The joy of the Lord is my strength."* Take joy in Me, in My promises, and in My never failing love for you. *"My God shall supply all my needs through Jesus Christ."* Trust in the Lord for He is faithful!

LAST DAYS

The very thought of self that My children have will bring an assault against them by sin, self, and or Satan. It is in these days that I mount up power to draw My children closer that the power of error in the world try's and all out effort to raise rebellion to a fever pitch! Be aware; be more careful and more cautious in all your ways. Learn by drawing Me closer to ask Me, and take more time deciding your way. Yes, learn to ask Me, wait upon Me, and seek Me more in all things. I am your helper, remember? By being obedient to the words I bring morning after morning I can draw you safely along Our way. It is the independent souls that I lose touch with! Where do you want to be? Out on your own now, in these times?

"Thy will be done in me and through me, oh Lord my strength and my redeemer." My child, have always an attitude of love. Know that My love is upon you. Be an ambassador of love to others. The more you share, the more I can pour out on you. Walk each day confidently, knowing that the Holy Spirit is leading you. He is your comforter release His blessings into your life. Enjoy the love, peace, and joy He has for you. Live in His goodness and patience. Rest in the faith he has put into your being. Let self-control from Him keep your life steady and smooth. Walk in God's righteousness always releasing His love and peace.

THE NEAR LAST CALL

The rights of man are truly few or nothing, it is because they are so desired that man will fight and die for "their rights." This is self fighting for more and more for self. If only these lost men would open their heart to Me I would give answer to all they desire! My rights that I give to My children far more surpass anything of man, yet man keeps away from Me. My dear ones, who know Me, seek after and find these self serving lost souls and bring them to Our salvation! All children I desire, but all children do not seek as they should, so you try to stir and waken them as I lead you! This is the team work of My heart that I desire. "save My lost ones." My call is to all My children for all of the time now left; keep your eyes open for My lost ones. I will lead you, guide you, and call them to you and for you. For the time is that short!

It is time to put your cares and worries in the hands of Jesus. Deposit them in His loving care knowing that He is able to bring about the right solution in all things. Keep in constant contact with him through prayer and meditation. *"And all things whatsoever ye shall ask in prayer, believing, ye shall receive."* Trust God for He is faithful. Walk the path He has provided for you. Keep your thoughts and words positive and pure for you can be snared by the words of your month. *"Let the words of my month and the meditation of my heart, be acceptable in thy sight, Oh Lord my strength and my redeemer."* Remember: God is light, in Him there is no darkness, so walk in His light, in

His love. Let God have His way in you for He loves you and is working for your good always.

TRUTH FACED

The twisting and turning that man does to escape his life seldom accomplishes any good, but it is the stopping and facing truth that will settle a thing. It is when truth is faced with a true desire to settle affairs that I can guide and support every effort. I am truth and every effort of man to work with truth causes My help. A help unseen, guidance without appearance, but My help none the less. Dear one listen to Me in your heart. Quiet and peace are the comforters of My doing, and I can be trusted in all your problems. Wait upon Me, call upon Me, and seek My face, will, and way. When you do We will find Our way together through all life can throw at you. Not hand in hand at first, for heart with heart must be Our start! Then hand in hand will always be Our way, walk, and talk! It is with persistence We are brought together, as love grows. Love grows as it flows from Me and you find your place of acceptance!

My Word is true, My promises are for you. "Thy *Word is a lamp unto my feet, and a light unto my path.*" Take His word into your heart and soul and make them a part of your being. Build your faith solidly on the Word of God. "*So then faith cometh by hearing and hearing by the word of God.*" You are to stand on The Word in all situations. God's will comes through His righteousness. "*But seek ye first the kingdom of God and His righteousness and all these things shall be added unto you*! Rise up, above all worldly situations and seek His face. He has the answer. Stand on His Word. "*All scripture is given by inspiration of God and is profitable for doctrine, for reproof, for correction, for instruction in righteousness.*"

MY HEART

This walk with "writing talk" is like none other in that I have poured out My heart more and more. This is truth that builds, truth that I seldom share freely. **This is a last time flow of truth for My last time achievers.** A helping hand that I seldom extend in such ongoing detail. You who read **these words of wisdom**, guidance, and helps give close heed to these things here said. These are truths of heavenly guidance most needed just before the catching away! How else can I achieve this desire of My heart unless someone will write these words I long to share with all of you who will stay with this outpouring of gold and silver pouring forth. Read and reread with loving care, believing will lead to achieving all I can pour into leak proof vessels of love. Note: "leak proof" means don't let it pour out unprofitably!

"The joy of the Lord is my strength." Go forward each day in peace knowing that you are a child of God and He has His hand on you. He is loving and guiding you into righteousness, and the joy that come from knowing the Lord. Be an over-comer for a way has been made. Jesus said, *"I am come that they might have life, and that they might have it more abundantly."* Walk daily in abundance for Jesus made it possible. Learn to rest in the Lord, to wait on Him, *"But they that wait in the Lord, shall renew their strength."* Have the blessed assurance that comes from knowing and trusting God in all things. God is love and He is faithful to watch over His children.

You think this earth life of yours goes on and on, but you haven't seen anything yet! Our on and on is in the always and forever category, never ending because there is always something to seek more and more! We have a forever walk of love expansion into realms of heaven not yet revealed or never even imagined! My plans are in the always and forever on-going type, from victory to victory, not over people, but wonder to wonder and great to greater. What a future I hold before My loved ones! Creations unrevealed of wonders never imagined! Oh, My dear ones there are not words sufficient to even touch on the what of things I hold for revelation! Still one step at a time must be Our walk into the plans of My heart for you! Keep always open to **revelation knowledge** now, for that is the method of expression of Spirit I desire you to grow into!

"Be still and know that I am God." Seek Me in all that you do. Have peace in your heart and love for all. Be covered in My love for I died to blot out your sins and release My love in you. You are soul and Spirit living in

a body. Open your heart to Me and My words to you. Let go of self and seek more of Me. Search My Word for truth and My directions for your life. *"Thy word is a lamp unto my feet, and a light unto my path."* Let My love lift you up and show the way. My way for you is filled with the joy of the Lord, and His peace and mercy and love forever. My child, *"Arise, shine for thy light is come, and the glory of the Lord is risen upon thee."*

TRUTH'S BEAUTY

The work of My hands must be displayed in all openness and truth! How else can I bring truth apparent if no child listens to Me and hears Me in their heart and responses? **Only your heart response is much sought and desired.** On this type of action all heaven, all angels, and I will move. Keep this truth ever before you for this is where Our whole eternity grows and expands in wonder and truth! Yes, I hold truth as the foundation for all My streets of gold! Jesus is truth does this fact not set truth surrounding My throne? Come dear ones see truth in all of the glory I give it! Is not truth My heart, My soul, My Son, and My all? Let all past, all now and all future, forever and always sing out truth in all of truth's beauty!

Do not look back, look forward, and press forward to lay hold of the promises I have for you. This is a new day. This is the day the Lord hath made, I will rejoice and be glad in it. Look expectantly toward each day for My presence and My blessings. Expect good things from the Lord for He loves you. See the Lord in others and let them see Jesus in you. *"Delight thyself in the Lord and He shall give thee the desires of thine heart."* Be happy always for you are a child of God, fashioned by Him in His love. He created you to be His perfect child and all things are working toward that end. *"He which hath begun a good work in you will perform it until the day of Jesus Christ."* Be happy knowing that "all is well."

DAYS OF VICTORY

All paths of man will never be paths of truth to follow. My dear children must learn to read My Word, the Holy Bible, and then learn to listen for My still soft voice. How long will I have to bring this simple truth out? Not too much longer now! Yes, time is running out on man, I am not running out on him. However I will not call and call forever when I have such wonders and truths to be exposed to My children who have turned, found Me, and We now walk together. Yes, "for always" is for them My chosen ones, My dear ones, My faithful dear children. Gather all those about you that know Me more and more as these final days flow by. For by so doing you will find more and more of My love being revealed and released. These are the budding days of victory. Learn to sense and feel that this is so. You will receive My forever blessing beginning to flow!

Lift up your dead and receive what the Lord has for you. Take to yourself the multitude of blessings He is offering you. Receive love, peace, and joy, patience, goodness and faith, even meekness and self control. These blessings are all available to you through the Holy Spirit God has given you. Take what is rightfully yours; and use it to the glory of God. Release this power from God into your life. Come to Me, dear children, draw closer so that We may be as One. I have peace, perfect peace for you, trust in Me! *"Thou will keep him in perfect peace, whose mind is stayed on thee, because he trusteth in thee.*" God's promise to you, enjoy living in His peace.

ABIDE IN ME

When I find a child of Mine who has eyes that see then I am able to display before him hidden manna of great worth. This then should be told and made clear to My dear ones who still seek and struggle to find My path of wonders. I hide nothing to hearts that are openly Mine in all they do. Now and always becomes real, and more real, as I open hearts to see and hear and have revealed My hidden wealth of knowledge for growth into My heart, life, and way. Where We go is not for all to know but truth revealed is what I show. The light I turn on is the heart knowledge that reveals truth in the Spirit to show revelations as I desire knowledge and wisdom to flow. What flows, who knows, but Spirit willingly tells and shows, and Spirit seeking fills and goes. This path is only clear to all My children who seek, listen, and hear. Abide in Me and you will have ears to hear and eyes to see. Release self forevermore and I'll take you to My far shore! Hear this call deep in your heart, and that will give a fresh start!

Let My love overflow in your heart. For in love, My love, you are strengthened and given peace and wisdom to live the life that I have put before you. Walk gently caring for others along the way. Show forth Jesus in your life that others may learn of His Love. You are My ambassadors, the Spirit of Jesus here on earth. *"Now stir up the gift within you."* Show forth the gift of love that has been given you. Remember My words; *"Fear nothing for I am with you, be not afraid for I am your God I strengthen you, I help you, I support you with My victorious right hand."* God's promise is true! If God be for us who can be against us? Rejoice His hand is upon you.

FOREVERMORE

When I finally set My children in their place they shall surely know and be glad forevermore! Yes, I make Israel My joy forever on the earth, and Our time will go on growing in My ways endlessly. My plan carries with it all necessary abundance to support the universe as I see fit. This is truly a dream I shall build on more and more, so all may share in everlasting through everlasting My glory expanding! Dear ones this that is written is but a simple casting of a picture that is only shown now in black and white, but has the great potential of full color forevermore!

Your Word is a joy unto my heart. Therefore, *"Let the words of my mouth and the meditations of my heart be acceptable in thy sight, Oh Lord, my strength and my redeemer."* May My thoughts be your thoughts and My words are your words, for My heart is filled with love for you. *"Draw nigh to God, and He will draw nigh to you."* Be in one accord, and let your desires be His desires, and truly seek His face. Live in peace with all men that God's love may show through you. Have a quiet Spirit, in peace and harmony with God's will. Truly I say to you, *"Let everything you do be done in love."* For God is love and love is the essence of all things!

GROWING ONENESS

Our walk will blossom forth in newness day by day. Truth will always be Our vehicle of movement, and beauty of love will provide comfort forever. Our time is endless and love ever expanding has a Spiritual depth of meaning never revealed before. Keep always believing more from love and love's display will show endearing wonders and surprises of My heart not dreamed of by man. Our growth in Oneness has never been explained or made clear in all of its ramifications for good reasons. Man cannot receive the plan of My heart for them while still in the blood flesh only in Our growing Oneness in the Spirit can this never ceasing blessing unfold itself. Only love growing in the Spirit of My dear ones will ever come to full display I desire. Give Me more and more of your time now and Our time will blossom in a growing newness and wonder day by day!

Rest in Me, rest in My love and I will lift you up. Take joy in Our time together. Be nourished by My words to you. Live and grow Spiritually, always with Me leading the way. *I am the way the Truth and the Life, no man comes to the Father but by Me.*" These are Jesus' precious words to His children. Jesus shows the way, He is the way. Work to be more like your Lord and Savior, Jesus. We are directed to, "Have the mind of Christ." My children remove the darkness in your life by taking in the light, Jesus. *"I am come, a light unto the world, that whosoever believeth on me should not abide in darkness.*" The Lord's promise to you "live in the light!"

THE WALK

The walk of My people has been well recorded for I hold their walk before "always." This is a record of the struggle of man, but not of man only for it shows My Son and Our work quite plainly. For one purpose only to bring forth My Son's story and Our great struggle with man making the eternity to be won one of great respect! Where every child comes from is from My heart, but where every child is destined to go is from their heart! Let no man miss My great purpose in all of this "My struggle" to bring forth "**My family of forever**." Yes, a family of forever is won only by great struggle. Why do I bring this forth now? Only to stop you and say, "Do not overlook Our whole work to bring each one of you who read this to NOW, for all this that has past is Our sure foundation of Our future to come!"

"Create in me a clean heart dear Lord," so that I may see you more clearly. Do seek the face of the Lord. Call upon the Holy Spirit within you to make things clear. The

Holy Spirit is a part of the God Head and has been given to teach, guide, and lead you into righteousness. Release this power and knowledge into your life for it is a gift from God to His children.

Allow God to use you for He has a perfect plan for your life. Let go of self so that there may be room for Jesus. Jesus comes into our lives as self is put down. *"Thy will be done, in me and through me oh Lord, my strength and my redeemer." "When I am weak, He is strong."* Trust in His Word, His promises to you for He is faithful!

TRUTH SEEKING

Yes, all of Our writing brings to My children the thoughts of My heart for them day by day. Learning comes to all who read, study, meditate and dwell on all that is said. My words are My words in whatever book they are presented. It is in knowing this truth that My children will find great benefit. Keep this thought always clear in your mind and heart for out of this can I bring many thoughts expanding. Only by truth seeking children does My Word cause benefit and worth to flow freely as I wish!

Keep careful watch over My words for where they go and what they do is of great importance to Me! Learn to re-read and regard them as jewels that sparkle differently in different light and times! My words are like tools that open understanding to bring blessings and worth to many, even in rare and new situations. Jewels give sparkle and light under many different circumstances, it is so also with My many words of truth and wisdom.

Walk in the abundant life that God has given you. Go forth with joy in your hearts, confident that He has made a way for you. Live and have your being in the light of the Lord. *"I am come, a light into the world, that whosoever believeth on me should not abide in darkness."* This is Jesus' promise to you, receive it and live your life in the light of the Lord. Be steadfast in His light and in His love. *"Let everything you do be done in love,"* for this is the will of the Lord for you. Rejoice in His love and His constant covering over you.

MY WAYS

The works of man are but repetitions of the works of evil men of the past. Learn My children about My ways of the past for I am the same yesterday, today, and tomorrow. The times of evil I am now loosening upon the earth once again for their foul ways have filled the lands. Once again evil flourishes and I must bring it all to a halt. My children are ready to leave, and I am getting ready to end Israel's time and start anew My ways for My dear ones. Yes, truly these times now are the beginnings of the end. Another end of an age, and then the setting up of the next one. I am eager to get on with it for these times ahead must occur to bring the Father's plans to fulfillment on time. Set right these times in your heart for truth will out and times will come to pass that must be. All that has been will come to pass and We will find truth to be a bearer of facts to be fulfilled. Out of it all the Father will have His family. The heavens are as fruit ripening on the vine and victories light is dim now but shinning will burst forth!

Start the day with praise and worship to the Lord. *"Let that mind be in you which was also in Jesus Christ!" "Be still and know that I am God." "Let His thoughts be your thoughts, His Words be your words."* Cast out thoughts of worldly problems or self, let

God's Word and His promises fill your soul. Take joy and peace and God's love into your heart and act accordingly. Show forth His love. Let others see His love in you. Be patient and have self control for this is His will for you. See others as God's children and you will see the good in them. Think on and dwell in the positive, in His light. He has brought you the light in His Son Jesus. Live in the light!

MY PEOPLE

These times just before you are to be as jewels that need care. Shine, polish, and preserve each day now for I am willing and ready to see works of love performed under Our hand. Believe for more and more, and I will see these things of Ours transpire! Go forth seeking for the places that I show you, for then Our walk can bring about My will and way day-by-day.

Believe for more, more, more children saved, more light shone in dark places, more truths exposed and more blessings flowing. Have a desire that I may fulfill, see more opportunities that come before you to show love. Start a talk that I might enjoy. Learn to see hearts in My people that I have put there. Come now and walk to the talk!

"My voice shall thou hear in the morning, oh Lord, in the morning will I direct my prayer unto thee, and will look up." Thank you Lord for hearing my prayers and answering them. This time of communion is an important bond between Us. Continue praying, continue being still, so that you can hear My voice; there is Spirit growth in the quiet time.

Let My words stir you up and change you. Be lifted up as your mind is stayed on Me. Be encouraged knowing that My love is enfolding you always. Live in peace, the joy of the Lord is yours. Take hold of My gifts to you and make them a part of your life. Live in peace, joy, and love and you will show others My way, and My love! Rejoice, for each day is a new beginning for you with Me.

SPIRITUAL GROWTH

Yes, when I speak to the heart of man sometimes I speak things difficult for him to face or to bare, but how else does truth come but by climbing the hill or cliff to reach the place of clear sight? To view things from My viewpoint is a privilege not to be ignored, but to be carefully considered. Have I not opened your eyes and heart to be more like Jesus? Have I not shown you My will and way in many things at different times? Are We not growing together in this walk of the Spirit?

The walk in the Spirit brings one to view many of man's things and ways from My heavenly viewpoint! Is truth uncomfortable? Yes, to wayward man, sometimes most uncomfortable but isn't heavenly growth worth it? The price to pay for the ticket to play is costly day by day. Only Spiritual growth is won slowly. Yes, even hour by hour!

"Surely goodness and mercy shall follow me all the days of my life, and I shall live in the house of the Lord forever," this is God's will for all of His children. Live in and receive His goodness and mercy. Know that it is always available to you. Reach out and take what is rightfully yours. As you receive these blessings of the Lord, send them forth to others. Be patient and understanding in all situations for God would have Us be kind

and gentle toward His children. *"Draw nigh to God, and he will draw nigh to you."* In your close walk with Him you will be filled to over-flowing with His love. Therefore, *"Let everything you do be done in love."* For this is the will of God.

WALKS WAY

Our walk and Our work are the same. As you go forth I go with you. As I decide We do, that is Our walk's way. Victory is Ours always as Our walk is together and satisfies all! This walk has begun and now must grow and manifest its self more day by day. Even as We go, We know and see things as One. This is the way of Our togetherness. Let this Oneness of way be made more real now day-by-day.

Walk in this as reality day by day and We will see and know together as We should. Begin to learn this as reality and I Will make it so. It is learning to live Our reality that the truth if it becomes manifested! Walk the walk of Our reality to make it so!

Lift up Jesus, in your actions, your words, and in your thoughts. In return He will lift you up to heavenly places and you will enjoy a new closeness with Him."*Let this mind be in you which was also in Christ Jesus."* You have within you the Holy Spirit, a gift from God. He has for you the fruit of the Spirit, which are promises from God.

Claim these promises for you are a child of God. Release them into your life and make them truly your own. Display love, and peace, and joy, so that others may see Jesus in you. Have complete faith that God is leading you. Be meek and gentle showing the goodness of God. Let God do the leading as you use the self-control God has given to you. You have all that you need to be a complete child of God. Rejoice and be glad in it!

MY LOVE FREE

This walk is sure to grow as attention is given. To let this walk flow will be as I am free to move and do more and more through and with you. This letting is the lesson to learn now. I am released more and more as We grow into togetherness of thought and being or doing. This is the way of self down, and Jesus up. Yes, let Jesus rise up and you will know what it is I'm speaking about now. Growing into the man I desire you to be means self down, and Jesus up. Does this seem strange? Well, it is until proper thought is given to what is just said. How else will I do My work in and through you unless self is released and Jesus freed? Oh you know what I mean! This is simply obedience to My Spirit in you, obedience to growing closer to this Oneness I speak of more and more. This is a goal of Oneness where We truly move with One heart and One mind. Only My will prevailing and My love free to move! *"Be still and know that I am God"* Quiet your soul and hear what the Lord has for you. Be renewed in this time, let the Father renew your Spirit and lift you up.

TRUTH OF WORTH

It is My truth written that I desire, for then I can make it available to whomsoever will believe! This, for these times, is the best We can do. Only My will made known for now is available in this or like manner. Where else or how else shall this be under taken? True believing is rare achieving in the environment of this day! By persistence will

We accomplish this setting of My truth in this earth place for now, My truth lives by dispersion for only truth sent forth to believers will bring the proper accomplishment required at this time. I will teach, guide, lead, and show only willing hearts with ears to hear, how else will I set this truth of worth to fulfill My desires of My heart? Now is the time of release required, now is the time, for

time I control, and time of Mine is the ruler of events of necessity. Now is time set as necessary to the unfolding of events of great conclusions!

"Arise, shine, for thy light is come, and the glory of the Lord is risen upon thee." Let your soul be filled with the light of the Lord. Chase away all darkness and let His light in. For when there is Light then can be no darkness. Look to God, Jesus, and the Holy Spirit for all direction. *"I am come, a light into the world, that whosoever believeth on Me should not abide in darkness."* Let His light lead you and lift you up. Know that Scripture is written for you: *"All Scripture is given by inspiration of God, and is profitable for doctrine, for reproof, for correction, for instruction in righteousness."*

Know Him and know His Word and others will be blessed by your light (God's light in you) and your love!

TRUTH OF ONENESS

Forever obey the will of Him who loves you and gathers you unto Himself. Jesus is His name and forever is His reign. All shall call His name wonderful, and forever shall He be! Jesus is the all in all and all His children shall be as He is forever. Forever is the kingdom of God's Dear Son and forever are His people with Him. Forever in Oneness, Forever in love, Forever is His kingdom of love. The Father is all in all and His Son reigns throughout always! There is an inconceivableness about God in which no man will come close knowing, even the inconceivableness of Oneness. Yes, the Oneness with man, and man with God, will never bring man to the truth of Oneness. God the Father is truly a Oneness alone! It is in His love only that He draws man into this Oneness with Him. God is far above, far beyond, and far in eternity with His Oneness where no man can go! This is the forever mystery of Oneness where no man can go!

Open your heart and hear the voice of the Holy Spirit. He will keep your life balanced and full. He is your source of all truth, as are the Scriptures. Receive and live in the fullness of truth and God's love. *"Thy word is a lamp unto my feet, and a light unto my path."* Walk in this light, have faith in the voice of the Holy Spirit. Know that, *"He which hath begun a good work in you will perform it until the day of Jesus Christ."* Trust in the Lord with all your heart for He is faithful and His love is everlasting!

FATHER'S LOVE

Yes, the Father of "all" invites His children as His family of partakers of the love which opens them to everlasting, unending, wonders of a rich wealthy and a giving God of everlasting "allness." This gift of family is never to be fully explained because the sum and total of it is never ending, never told, for it is too much for words to convey. Even the nearness of it is too much for any clarity to be revealing enough. The unending of it will leave no time sufficient for explanation! My dear ones trust only will carry you always in safety to live and see the total of Our Oneness with this ongoing reality of the Father's love. Let that love now be the all of your need for each day given. Live always with My nearness sufficient for all your wants, needs, and cares. Live always in the sufficiency of Our love!

Go forward, reaching toward the Lord and His righteousness. For, *"Blessed is the man who perseveres under trials, because when he has stood the test, he will receive the crown of life that God has promised to those that love him."* Jesus said to keep on asking, to keep on seeking, and to keep on knocking. We are to push toward the goal, be an over-comer, and rise above the stumbling block that may be before us. God is with you, and you have the Holy Spirit helping you, but you must step out. You must take that first step, and then the Lord will come along beside you and make a way. Trust that He is with you always. You are to grow Spiritually by pushing forward toward His righteousness in love and peace.

KINGDOM RULERS

In the various affairs of man I watch over, but don't interfere, because the unfolding there of interests Me. However the affairs of My children are dear to My heart. It is in their freedom of growth they attain the self worth needed to fully develop the dear ones I love. This is why you find Our walk seeming to progress without My detail guidance. Does this insight give you comfort in the life We will have together? Yes, I always have and always will guard, watch over, and protect, but I do not wish to move you as My puppets. When We come into Our complete Oneness then all will be different, for your inheritance frees you as kingdom rulers. Have I not said you are My priests and kings? Come dear ones grow in this understanding of who you truly are becoming!

My Blessing covers the earth. Each one must receive this blessing and live in it if it is to be effective. *"My sheep hear My voice"* Truly if you desire to be a child of God you will hear His voice, you will accept Him in your heart. You will live a life in righteousness, constantly drawing closer to God and His precepts. The Holy Spirit, a gift from God, is your teacher. He will release blessings into your life as you desire them. Let prayer, worship and meditation be your life-line to God! *"But seek ye first the Kingdom of God, and His righteousness and all these things shall be added unto you."* Rest in the Lord knowing always He is a God of love and His righteousness is covering you.

MY HANDS

It is with time in teaching, I bring a child of Mine into knowledge and understanding I desire him to possess. Yes, you can use the Holy Scriptures given you below to satisfy this work of Ours. We together are bringing truths that I desire for those children who I bring to these books of Ours. This is teaching from My hands as I desire. How or when I put this work to great display is also at My time, will, and way. Your part now, and has been and is, to read and use these words. We are seeing this as satisfactory work being done. My appeal through this method is unusual, never the less it is as I desire. This is a release of truth flowing I deem wanted and necessary now, at this time. It is with My permission this word here given may be used to whoever doubts or questions Our efforts! The following Holy Scriptures are here given to cover what has been written in these books. II Cor.

5:18-20; II Cor. 2:14-17; II Cor. 3:5-12; &
17,18; John 16:13-15; Isa. 50:4,5.

"As many as are led by the Spirit of God, they are the sons of God." Truly you are a child of God, a part of the family of God. Rejoice, for Jesus made this possible by His shed blood, giving up His life that you may be cleansed from all sin. Therefore, walk as a child of God. Loose the wonderful blessings into your life from the Holy Spirit. They are for you, to teach, nurture, strengthen, and guide you into all righteousness, Let the joy of the Lord be your strength. Abide in His wonderful Love and be at peace with all men. Walk confidently knowing that, *"He which hath begun a good work in you will perform it until the day of Jesus Christ."* Walk in His way, in His light with joy in your heart. Live an abundant life for Jesus said, *"I have come that they might have life and that they might have it more abundantly."*

BELIEVE

This day shall be a day that possesses, in glory and wonder, the works that I speak for I hold back My hand of blessings until My purposes have fulfilled their mark and made their desires clear. Yes, there must be a confrontation come for all things well and good to be made clear. Just as a day dawns like any other, but such then occurs to make plain a great change has happened. Look now to new things being stirred and awakened. Yes, seek and find My hand showing a turn around, a change of direction. Believe that new has come, and then We can go into bigger and better things.

SPECIAL PATH

When the stirring in a man's soul becomes a driving force in him to find more of Me and Mine, then I have a child growing into the dear one I will draw closer and closer all of the time. Learn to read these truths I bring you with understanding, for only by My leading will you find the true path I desire for you. Keep always open and seeking, for only then can I open your special path of learning that I desire for you. Never feel that I am too much because I am only releasing little-by-little the path you would never find by your own efforts. It is only by believing in My leading that there will be any leading given.

Be still, look up, and seek My face for the answers to life's problems. Go through every situation holding My hand, listening to My voice. You have been redeemed by the blood of Jesus. You are now covered in My love and peace, so have the joy that is yours. Remember: the Holy Spirit now dwells within you and it is He who knows the will of God. He was sent to aid you in being all that God has designed you to be and to have all God wants you to have. Receive all the blessings and walk in His Love always.

TRUE BEGINNING

Our daily walk must now always be! This is your **true beginning**__with Me. Most children never come to a closeness that I desire, but it is the way of fruitfulness to grow forever. For you to keep these words I bring close to your heart will prove of tremendous worth in your future. You are building foundations that can carry worthwhile living. Every child of Mine will grow closer just because of Our togetherness, however close. It is the willingness and desire of heart that continues to build the love of Ours I desire. Sincerity of purpose, measures the depth of

love. It is heart or Spiritual growth that I count as a true barometer of love. All this I now give is true help worth doing. Even the trying to do I can enhance! Truth, these kinds of truth, is the stepping stones to the heaven of great ongoing! I have many
places just right for every dear one who makes himself Mine! Keep this ever before you for only as your desire becomes My desire can Our desire inspire growth evermore to great advantage building.

Thank you for Your grace that covers us in all situations, Your grace carries us through. It is our help in over-coming and putting things behind us. It is the love, peace, and joy of Jesus that carries us over and through the difficulties. Thank you Lord, for walking with us always. You show the way, You are our strength. You make a way for us when all seems dark. You are the light of the world. Your love builds us up and gives us strength and courage to go forward. Help us to walk in Your light, and in Your love, until we can be with You forever.

MY WORD

Rereading and rereading is building and growing on a solid foundation of love I bring. Time spent in this way pays off day-by-day. Keep always your feet on the ground I have prepared, and you will be climbing the stairs I have prepared! Spiritual growth generally comes in spurts of growth. The why of this is because man can stand just so much at a time! True learning is slow growing, but this is as I desire, for then it becomes a more forever blessing. This drawing of man closer to the Spirit realm becomes the major testing of a man allowing Me to choose the ones I desire to draw into a closer walk with Us. Eternity is a gift that should be more readily accepted, but man has the sex, sin, and self problem to defeat. Why do I set these hindrances? Isn't it reasonable for Me to have difficult barriers to prevent later obstacles and hindrances in eternity by setting walls or barriers that weed out potential intrusions later on?

My Holy Scriptures tell you to seek, ask, and knock and you will find. You will find the glorious promises of God to His children. You will know the will of God in your life and you will be shown God's plan to walk and live righteously. Seek His face, have regular communication with the Father through Jesus in worship and prayer. He is with you always so enjoy His presence. Draw upon it to fill your needs and give you strength, and to show the way. Let His love enfold you, live and have your being in His peace, and experience the joy of the Lord every day. Be lifted up out of heaviness and into the light. Overcome life's obstacles by being one with the Lord. Receive all the blessings He has for you and rejoice. Give Him praise!

HEART AND PURPOSES

This that is written for Me daily will become a work well done to great purpose. The words I bring carry My heart and purposes as I desire them to be shown. I encourage this to stay to complete My expressions of guidance I desire to give. These details are from My heart to fulfill My wishes that are shown. As I have said before, and I say again now, **"It is most necessary, yes even imperative that I deliver to my dear ones words of guidance for use in their daily growth."** My Holy Bible gives such guidance in many parables and stories, but in this method I am able to give more direct assistance to each individual who comes to this way for proper obedience training. All will grow into usefulness only when they know and are shown just what I require. My dear ones use this work and I will be a guide and helper to each one who responds eagerly and purposefully!

Rest in the Lord for He has made all things possible. Go forward doing the work He has for you, but rest while doing so. See yourself strong in the Lord, empowered to do the things He has for you to do. He sees you as freed from sin, strong and able. Relax in His love and grace. Remember: *"Thy will be done, in me and through me Oh Lord, my strength and redeemer."* Live in His rest, in His glory, and in peace for this is the will of the Father toward you.

THIS ONENESS

Our walk is Our work together, and in this manner Our love grows. No other course is better suited to bring this Oneness I seek with all of My children. Keep in mind that I have many ways to draw My loved ones into a walk suited properly for each one. Remember judge not, especially do not try to speculate about how I am drawing any other child of Mine, for your view of these things will be as if it were from the bottom of a very deep well! All are special, all are held in high regard by Me no matter what you may think. Another reason for your poor position for judging anyone is My timing for them. You have no platform for viewing between your time and their time. Let love for others is on this no judging at all platforms! A love walk will lift you up as no other way can!

You have been cleansed and made ready for a new day. Do not carry baggage over from day-to-day. Each day is sufficient unto its self. Live one day at a time earnestly doing the will of the Father. He gives you strength and wisdom for one day at a time. Always keep in close contact with God through prayer and praise and worship. Be convinced that, *"My God shall supply all my needs according to His riches in glory, through Jesus Christ."* Rest in that promise for He is a faithful God filled with love and peace. He will make all things possible for that day as long as you stay in His will. Receive the covering of glory and peace He has for you and walk in it each day. *"Surely goodness and mercy shall follow me all the days of my life: and I shall dwell in the house of the Lord forever."*

The timing of a man's walk with Me is left to him, for I in no way force or draw strongly any who lack the desire for Me. Wouldn't it be foolish to entice, push, or pull anyone to come into your party when their intent later would be to spoil all you have provided for your guests? This cannot be made or said too strongly, I draw no one into My forever with Me who does not show a **strong willful desire** to be with Me! **This dear ones is your word most important!** Take care about how much you give your heart to Me. If it is not your "whole heart" I don't want it!

How could heaven be happy with half hearted children? See that your desires are My desires; My desires are your desires. See? Bring Our desire for Our Oneness to be equal to My desire for Our Oneness, forever is a long, long time! Even your trying with the best you can, I will know and honor! Truth will come out!

"This is the day that the Lord has made, I will rejoice and be glad in it." Live in the grace of God for it enables you to live a holy

life. Today represent the Lord in all you do. You are a child of God so favor your Father by your love one to another. Let His glory shine through you so others may know the love of Jesus. Rise up and be strong in the Lord for truly, *"The joy of the Lord is your strength."* Allow His peace to flow through you. Go through this day in perfect peace. In this way the Lord can use you to minster to others. Remember: the glory of the Lord is your covering.

GOD'S LOVE

Rise up and be a light for the Lord. The love Jesus has poured into you is to be channeled out to others. In any way possible show forth the love of the Lord. Overcome the obstacles of self or of the world, and let God's love show the way. God tells you, *"For my yoke is easy; and my burden is light."* Share all things with the Lord, under His direction, and He will make a way. His Way is not a burden but a joy. *"And let us not be weary in well doing for in due season we shall reap, if we faint not."* Keep your eyes on Jesus and He will make a way!

When I speak to My loved ones I give a special message from My heart. I will speak of truths that lead guide and draw closer those who have ears to hear. **This is the first and most important method of Our communication** while you are still in the flesh. Only words of up lifting truth are given at these times. I can open up the path of truth most necessary for all or any who are so open to Me and My ways. This is the most direct and easiest method of communication for these times, and by this method I can still the desire growing in each ones heart for this drawing closer all My dear ones should have in their hearts. **Only by hearing My truths well enough to write them down** can I be sure of their ability to obey Me.

This listening brings Our walk into a truth place of openness that is special and most important to each ones steps into their eternal walk that I have set for them in ages past. Yes, all this that is now being lived out is but the truth in action that My heart has planned in ages past. Have I not said you were with Me from the beginning in My heart? A record of Our doings is required by Me for all I do I put down for ages to come. This is My desire and My purposes are My own. Every child has a role given, for Our work is the work of unfolding throughout eternity.

The reasons for all I do, have done, and will do are all set in My heart for My pleasure only. The time of My things carry on in truth exposed as proof of My desires set in reality. All this is speaking of the life eternal already desired now being released in an everlasting reality of truth. My release of the heavens seen is but a small part showing of the reality of all My existence throughout the yet hidden realms of truth never to be known. My size is unfathomable. Our pastures to roam are indiscernible to man. Even Our forever is never to be shown because there isn't a way or method yet given. These things here said are not usual, but are intended only to show the unbelievable to those who still won't see!

Make each day a new start with Me and I can see that it is truly what it will be! I have no end of things to bring alive in the hearts of My children each day. A walk can become a garden of wonders on earth for each one whose ears are truly open listening for My words of guidance and encouraging love. Everyone is open to this word daily just for them. I have a wonder of truth to unfold that can touch the hearts of My listening ones daily. Truth, My truth unfolding is the walk for My listening ones who I hold so dear! Hear daily My words for you and I can draw you, each one, into Our forever so much quicker than you can believe for it. Just try Me and see!

See yourself as God sees you. Let the Holy Spirit rise up in you and release the blessings He has for you. Put self aside and allow God to do His work in you. Let the love of God overflow in your life. *"Give thanks unto the Lord, for He is good: for His mercy endureth for ever."* Let His mercy bring rest to your soul. *"Be still and know that I am God,"* and the peace that passeth understanding will enfold you. *"I will say of the Lord, He is my refuge and my fortress: my God; in Him will I trust."*

OUR LOVE FLOW

The overall care given to My children will never be known in its fullness. Why? Because it is too much, to detailed, so sweet and caring. Love has no bounds, no completion; therefore, it too is too much! Let your love for one another be so. Let Our love flow from your heart daily to touch those around you without thought of it about yourself. Love is to flow through you to others, when properly done it is only My love moving through you as My beloved vessel! The glory of it is mine, from Me through you as My beloved One! Keep self out of this work it is Ours and Ours alone. This is the walk of love, attain this and yours will become your victory forever! Walk with Me wherever you go and you will have the ongoing blessings for Our eternity!

PLACE OF BALANCE

My Holy Bible that I have given to My children is My way of introduction into the world of the Holy Spirit. This Spirit world is

My place of all forever. It is a place of truth only truth. Only what I show My children is truth, anything not of true truth is only the underside of all things. This "underside" is only the opposite of good. All My things are only of good, balance in all things requires that both sides be real, but the reality does not have to be open and made alive in My realm. If there were no darkness how would light show forth? If there is a top side there must be a bottom. In My Spirit realm only light is shown, but darkness must stay and keep the balance. This My dear ones, is reasonable for only perfect balance brings perfection of desire. To reach My place of balance is your way of Spirit growth. To reach safe haven forever you must be found to be *JUST LIKE ME.*

SPIRIT AND LIGHT

Surely My mercy and goodness will cover the lives of My children as they are taught, and as they learn to come to Me in Spirit and truth. There is no life outside of truth. Outside of truth is darkness, outside of truth all are lost forever! My children seek only truth, seek, strive for, and find My truth. Those who find Me will know Spirit and truth. There is no darkness in Spirit and truth. All My children shall dwell in Spirit and in light. All life everlasting is only in Spirit and light. I am the light of the world and heavens above and all about. Tell My children, you who are the light of the world now, for you are to spread this light wherever you go. Yes, you who know Me and are Mine spread My truth, be My light, show My truth as you can wherever you are.

"But seek ye first the kingdom of God, and His righteousness and all these things shall be added unto you." Have an attitude of love and kindness. Keep a mind of peace at all times. Let not your heart be troubled for God loves you. *"Let this mind be in you which was also in Christ Jesus."* When your mind becomes clouded in darkness purpose to bring in God's light, for it is always available

A LIVING KNOWING

This system that man has of believing must be improved and become a living knowing that dwells inside of every child of Mine. Keep in mind I sent My Holy Spirit to indwell the born-again child of Mine, but each one who asks must **believe and receive** forever this gift by his "knowing." The proof of believing then is shown by the use being made of My indwelling One. Yes, "God" indwells every born-again believer forever! This gift then either becomes used or useless. My dear ones wake up to truth! You are the gifted ones, each one of you but how many are true believers achieving? I have set up every child of Mine to be "My Jesus" where they are! Why don't I see this happening? ***Poor teaching,*** My true teachers must be Spirit-filled, moved by the Spirit, obedient to My Spirit, and be My anointed ones. When will this ever be? Never in the flesh for all, only will those who "know Me" well enough to obey and be led by Me can I trust! Each of you must judge yourself and make of you the best you can be!

"This is the day the Lord has made, I will rejoice and be glad in it." Direct your thoughts toward the good. The Lord tells us to think on the good; *"Finally brethren, whatsoever things are true, whatsoever things are honest, whatsoever things are just, whatsoever things pure, whatsoever things are lovely, whatsoever are lovely, whatsoever things are of good report, if*

there be any virtue, if there be any praise, think on these things." Keep your mind, your thoughts on Jesus and His love. If dark thoughts cloud your thinking immediately cast them out and let the pure thoughts of the Lord replace them. You are in charge, make a conscious effort to fill your mind with thoughts God would like. *"Arise, shine, for the Glory of the Lord is come upon thee."* This glory brings truth, goodness, joy and love. Let your thinking reflect His glory.

PERMENATE PLACE

When you are faithful to our morning meetings you are setting your permanent place at my right hand, forevermore! Do not now or ever guess or wonder about your place with Me. I speak My truth only to ears who hear and "know." **See that this is not a secret kept still or kept quiet!** All My children of obedience have this blessing to live by and live with! The wonders of Our walk are as the wonderful walk every child of Mine shall enjoy! Why are not all My children now enjoying these blessings I am speaking of? Because they won't listen to Me or listen to those who know and do for Me! Oh how I would that all ears be opened to hear My truth that I desire to pour out into dear hearts I love so much! Never stop, never be still but continue to pour out My truths to all. Yes, all who will listen and hear for they will either be blessed or come into condemnation by what their response is! What more can I ask, except to throw truth against the wall of unbelief daily until comes the end!

"Let everything you do be done in love." "Draw nigh to God, and He will draw nigh to you." My child, when you draw nigh to Me you are bathed in My love. Drawing close to Me is living in love and peace and joy. Stand fast against the evils of the world and self. Allow the light to chase out the darkness in your life. Where there is light, God's light, there can be no darkness. Be confident, knowing that God is your Heavenly Father and He loves you. Lean on Him and He will lead you into joy and peace. Walk through the valleys steadfast holding tight to Jesus knowing that He will see you through.

TRUTH RELEASED

The attempts to interpret My Word must clearly be under My leading. Man's efforts in his own strength and knowledge flounder around My truth; but I will assist and make clear any true effort. It must be timely and with My permission. Truth only flows at truth's proper timing and as I desire. To become My source of truth you must know My proper time of release for some truth carries great and extreme occasions of occurrences that I release and set upon the earth and its people! You have set upon such a reference in Scripture that I am speaking of. Yes, Isaiah 18 is a great and true exhibit of the changes about to occur on earth touching the whole world! Yes, it is a good place to make a release of truth about Isaiah 18. Pursue this and I will open your understanding for much truth is hidden and buried, and this has been kept closed for a long time!

I live in you in the Holy Spirit, My grace, My power, love and peace are all within you and available to you. Release all the blessings I have for you in the Holy Spirit. Live in My power, let My love flood your life and enjoy walking in perfect peace, My peace. *"Peace I leave you, my peace I give unto you: not as the world giveth, give I to you. Let not your heart be troubled, neither let it be afraid.*" Jesus' words, His promise to His children. Walk in His peace, His gift to you."*Thou will keep him in perfect peace, whose mind is stayed on thee, because he trusts in thee.*" Rest in the Lord for truly He is your source of all peace, love, power and joy.

CLOSER AND CLOSER

The calling of My children is always and ongoing! I am pleased when I have My dear ones with Me now and forever! This is truly ongoing and even into the end of an age and the beginning of a new one. It is with these times that I am drawing My dear ones closer and closer. See that all who you meet have this message made clear to them. The times demand this closer and closer walk. Call all who will listen, all who will hear with understanding, this door of Mine is opening wider and wider as the time draws nigh. This is not *as usual* but is mounting up to be *a great end time event*! Allow God's love to strengthen and keep you. Lean on Him for He is your strength and your peace. Be drawn into a closer walk with Him for this is His desire for you.

Our work never dims but is meant to be a light to My children. My words are truly Mine. Never doubt this that We are now doing. I find this work pleasing and I will make My words most useful to My children. Your part is to put these truths I bring out to My children, so they may see, feel, handle and know it is real! Just read on as you have been, Yes, I will bring help. These times are bringing more and more confusion and difficulty, but I have set a path, and will make a way through it all! Stay focused, stay steady, and just keep on! This walk is now day by day, hour by hour, and soon to be minute by minute. This age is fast coming to its planned completion and I will keep My will and way clear before My people. Truth will spring forth and time will prove out My Holy Bible truths are ever active!

My strength is your strength. Stay close to Me and I shall supply your needs. Remember: *"Trust in the Lord with all your heart, and lean not on your own understanding. In all your ways acknowledge Him and He shall direct your paths*." Rest in the Lord, being confident that He loves you and is taking care of you. Keep your mind stayed on Jesus and His light, for the darkness of the world is ever present. Guard you soul and heart against this darkness and live in the light of the Lord. Reflect God's light, let it shine faith to others, that they may see Jesus in you. Stay close to your Lord and you will be renewed daily, for He is your strength and peace and surrounds you with His mighty love.

A TRUTH WALK

Yes, We are now entering a most revealing time for My children. Yes, truth must prevail and few are there that will face My facts I am now opening. Truth is not just something nice all of the time just as truth of the cross shows. However truth also is the only path I give My dear ones to walk. This revelation for this day is showing what must be walked through to reach My goals I give to My worthy ones: some through the fire, some over the mountains, some in the caves, and overseas waves. My paths are varied and My trials are real, My children are given trials they feel: some I walk with, some have canes, some I carry and many are maimed, but through it all I draw the dear ones who hear My call. Come have no doubts do not stall; I am with you through it all!

Be ye steadfast, trusting in My Word, My promises to you. *"He that dwelleth in the secret place of the most high shall abide under the shadow of the Almighty. I will say of the Lord, He is my refuge and my fortress, My God; in Him will I trust."* God Our loving Heavenly Father will protect us; will keep us safe for we are His children. Rest in this knowledge. *"The Lord is my shepherd, I shall not want, I will fear no evil for thou art with me. Surely goodness and mercy shall follow me all the days of my life and I will dwell in the house of the Lord forever."* Stand on the promises of the Lord! Live your life covered in His love and His peace! You have been redeemed!

BEAUTY OF TRUTH

It is good when We clear up the prophetic written Word. Yes, this word in Isaiah 18 has all sorts of ramifications! There are simple explanations and then there are deep purposes to be explored. For now give only the simple obvious revelations. My Word, the Holy Bible, is filled with these types of words, but few are there who will spend time with Me enough to air out all that My heart desires to be revealed. The beauty of truth that is buried brings many children closer to My heart when with persistence and with fervor they continue inquiry until I reveal truth hidden. This will become My ongoing blessing to all those who do seek and seek until they find! Teach these lessons to all I put before you, how else can I give help to My seeking ones when no one will encourage and give guidance to them? Yes, I have a few who are pursuing My words as you are, but they too are seldom free and brought to the children's attention. Just know I am pleased as these truths are pursued.

Rest in the Lord for His love is restoring and renewing you. Walk in the path He has prepared for you. Stand tall and upright for, *"The joy of the Lord is your strength." "I have come that they might have life, and that they might have it more abundantly."* This is God's promise to His children. He is faithful to His Word. Be steadfast for the time is short and you shall be translated into the kingdom of light. Now you are to overcome the evil in the world and walk in the light. Stay close to Me and I will lead you through the darkness and into the light. Be strong in the Lord and My love will carry you through. I will save My children from destruction! *"Blessed is the man who perseveres under trial because when he has stood the test he will receive the crown of life that God has promised to those who love Him."*

THE FIRE

Yes, the time now set before My children is the final trials and testing times for the body of Christ. All must go through the fire. Jesus came to be like you, now you must come to be like Jesus. I never promised all an easy walk, but I did promise I will be with you. All of this now coming about is the refining, cleansing, healing, and restoring. All of the things I will bring you through are for your good! Let everything draw you closer to Me. Give Me all your time as soon as you can, thus making your walk the most fruitful one! ***Can you become like Jesus?*** Can you too walk the walk and talk the talk like Jesus? What do you think I mean when I say We shall be one, be like Jesus? Tried, yes, but only for your future benefit. Tested, only to find your best position in My kingdom. I do none of these things without Our purpose to be served. I am with you always.

In all things give thanks to your Heavenly Father. Focus your thoughts on what you have, not on what you don't have. *"Whatsoever things are true, honest, just, pure, lovely, of good report, any virtue or praise, think on these things."* Your words speak what the mind thinks. *"Let the mind be in you that was also in Christ Jesus."* Cast out all negative thoughts, critical thoughts, and ungodly thoughts for they are of the darkness. Open your mind and let God's light in. *"Let the words of my mouth, and the meditations of my heart, be acceptable in thy sight, oh Lord, my strength, and my redeemer.* Live in the light, perfect light of love!

MY NOW

Yes, this revelation is so on-going and important to Me that I will certainly open up more and more that can bring help to My children now! This area is so pivotal in the lives of the children of My now. This is truly a great time of separation just as the parable of the 10 virgins indicates. This knowledge should shake and wake the sleeping ones, the lazy ones, Yes, awaken many who think to no purpose about the times they live in. Yes, I will snatch many away if they will only open their heart and mind to Me now. This is not to be overlooked, forgotten, put aside or thought unimportant! How can I emphasize this more? We will keep drawing more and more attention to the times that now sit in the midst of the end Isaiah18.

"Thy will be done in me and through me, oh Lord my strength and redeemer." Listen always for the voice of the Lord, for His directions for your life. Live in a state of thanksgiving for God's blessings in your life. Keep your mind stayed on Jesus and His love. Live your life filled with His love, His peace, and His joy. These blessings are available to you because His Holy Spirit is within you and He has love, peace, and joy for you. They are the fruit of the Holy Spirit. Receive all God has for you so you may be a blessing to all others. Focus on the good and positive things, and let your words reflect the thoughts of your heart. Always see the good in others and in every situation. Rest in the Lord and let Him lead the way.

TELL TRUTH

Yes, tell truth; it is Our only hope. It must prevail; no other way will get you to the Father's heart! This should be a blessing, a wakeup call to My dear ones I love so much, but they have not been properly taught. My pastors have failed teaching My Son's Bride. Come now and make this a joyous time for I will draw all who will turn around and seek Me with their true heart now! This can be a saving revelation, try to make it so. I will help; I will open hearts to receive truth. Only truth My truth will bring My true children home. Tell the truth no matter what!

My child, walk in the blessing. The blessing I have prepared for you. Keep your eyes on Jesus and on My Word. Listen for the directions of the Holy Spirit. My love, My presence will keep you safe and guide you through all things. Surround yourself with My presence and fear not for I am with you always. Truly let the, *"Joy of the Lord be your strength,"* and then rest in Me. I will lift you up and carry you through. Let my love be the power in your life. Show forth My love to all, be My witness in a dark world. Never doubt My presence, so walk in complete peace. Be one with the Lord. He will make a way.

HEART TRUTH

Many will come in My name speaking well sounding words but only what I say to My children will stand. These times are, and will be, times of great confusion and upset, trials and testing. Keep always listening to Me in your heart; tell My children how important this is at this time. Not everything that sounds so right is to be believed. Great care is needed in these times, that is one of the reasons I released Isaiah 18 at this time, stick to what My Word has said! That word is a word to be trusted, the word to be believed and let it be the only way you go. You must draw My dear ones into the way of Our Holy Bible with Me speaking truth in their hearts. This is of great importance at this time. Many confusions pour forth, many false teachers and prophets will be crying out. Heed them not! My children must hear Me in their hearts, and follow only Me, for I am their voice of safety, their pathway to My heart. Continue to draw them to John 6:45. Continue to read Our truths. We are leading on the only biblical path to follow! *"**Learn to be like Jesus.**"*

"Arise, shine, for the glory of the Lord is risen upon thee." Go forth expressing that glory and the love of Jesus to all people. Be a light in a dark world and allow the people to see the light in you. Let Jesus and the power of the Holy Spirit be radiant in you. *"Let everything you do be done in love,"* according to the Scriptures. *"Now stir the gift within you."* The gift from God is the Holy Spirit and He is filled with blessings for all who will receive them; blessings of love, peace and joy, patience, self- control, goodness and faith. The world is so needy and hungry for this fruit of the Holy Spirit in their lives. Be a giver of hope in Jesus and the love He has for His children.

READY, PICK

Study Isaiah 18 to know its interpretation, for it ends on a dire note because its purpose is to set a startling end to a hard time. Seek the truth here given for it is for these people today for these times. This was "broad brush" words given in those early times. I have the right to save all My children any way I can, and now I see hearts ready for change so I call them quickly before the end. This is what all My children should know about these times. If any of you who read this work and know these times now have opportunity to further this work do it! As Isaiah 18 said, when the bud is ready, the vine is ready for picking. So PICK!

I call the bottom of your feet the soul of your feet. I call that the soul because that is where you should keep your soul *Under You.* You are Spirit, your Spirit is in your heart. I am in your heart and I work My will for you through your heart. Always keep your soul under your heart. Yes, the bottom of your feet is properly called soul! That is where it belongs!

I have given you the Holy Spirit and His power to enrich your life. Release and take advantage of this wonderful gift. This blessing is to draw you closer to Me and to fill your life with righteousness and light. The Scriptures tell you to *"Have the mind of Jesus Christ."* This mind is filled with goodness and love and the light of the Lord. Do not focus on the darkness of the world but on the light that is in Jesus. *"Rise, shine, for thy light is come, and the glory of the Lord is risen upon thee.*" Also remember God's Word, *"God is light, and in him is no darkness at all.* Seek the face of God, live in His love, and in His light!

REAL WALK

When will all this on-going work end? Never, if your walk with Me doesn't bring you closer to Me through all that you do, then you're walking in the wrong direction! Yes, this truth is *Truth Soul Shaking* until the reality of Our walk is *Real.* Make sure your walk is making Our walk a reality in your walk now! Just think about where you will be going in Our forever together! Yes, pay attention to these things I'm leading you to, because as you follow up in obedience We will see many things I desire for you to follow. Keep striving for more because the door has not been opened but a small a small crack up to now. I don't tell, demand, or push; it is only your walk you walk until My hand is completely shown. This is only to show what's yours as you move and grow. If you stop and stay that is alright it's your way!

"When you are weak He is strong." Rest in the lord and let Him lift you up. *"The joy of the Lord is your strength."* Believe that God is doing a work in you. Let your faith make a difference, rise up and claim the promises in the Scriptures, His promises to you. *"But seek ye first the kingdom of God, and His righteousness; and all these things shall be added unto you."* Walk in the abundant life the God has for you!

I CALL

This work is Mine, and I call the children to come and gather together with Me in all I endeavor. Yes, unless I call My dear ones who will know? Unless they listen, how will they know? It is each ones task to listen and to obey, how else can I build My kingdom? First pray that it is My will to do this that you seek, then wait upon Me for the when and how. The heart that is willing must first be the one that is called. I have many workers and many ways to go, but all is in My time. Obedience is the only sure path all must walk, and it is the most difficult to walk alone. Together is *Our only path.* Seek this each day before you do and then I will lead you through!

UP AND DOWN

Our walk has many ups and downs; this is as it should be, beware when everything just goes nicely all the time that too could be a path going astray! Expect to reach hard spots and also the easy going times. Just as life is so is Our walk! Are We not going along with each other the best We can? I can't give you too much too soon. You can't give Me too little too often. Yes, there must be a balance in this walk until the cliffs and the hard paths have reached the upper ground. Though I may know all about you, you can't know enough about Me! To grow and form and build and try is the best way lessons are learned. The hard ground will carry the load faster and safer! The hills and mountain roads will carry you higher and higher; think about that!

NEW DAY

All that I say will not happen in a day, but as My children cease their play they will draw their new day. Yes, every day can build or just let things waste away. Learn My dear ones from My simple rhymes, and then you'll make the perfect climb. All that appears to be must change to truth for you to see. Our walk is like a sea of glass that rain can shatter with a blast. When all is over I'm still there showing you new things to share. Take a walk, new each day, while We talk you'll see and stay. For with Me all comes in peace 'tell all your worries find release. This walk is new day by day opening truths to learn and say. Never lost, never the same, learning new truths to claim. See with your eyes; hear with your ears, wonders of truths will appear. You shall know the things through truth that will last and last. Yes, My truths build and grow, showing dear ones all they should know.

SOME DAY

Yes, my children must read My Word as I teach them; I only bring truth to the ears of my listening ones. Why? Who else is worth the effort? If my children who say they love me will not even try to listen to Me personally, how can I teach personally those who won't listen to Me? Oh, I won't lose them for as time in Spirit is on-going they will stir themselves some day! My dear ones are those who, while in the flesh of earth give time to Me in the Spirit. Our meetings with them can bear much fruit, and I can see clearly who I can give My trust. Do you see the worth of now doing this reading as I give words release I desire you to know? Say, "Yes, Lord! I am so grateful that you have made this work clear to Me." All are truly blessed to receive such wonders that are written down as these are. Just say, "Thank you, Jesus!"

TIME NOTED

Our on-going must be an on-going of forever. Draw closer and closer as I speak day-by-day for Our time is noted and shall be worthwhile! Our time is the only glue that holds Us together for no other way can bring the growth and improvement that is of growing worth. Say, Yes, Lord more and more to the Father as you see the great day dawning, and thank Him more for these morning times you have with Him and thank Him for His encouraging words each day!

It is with Our togetherness that We bond tight, only in that way will your growth and elevation come about. This is how the mysteries are solved; this is the result of Spiritual bonding. Spiritual bonds are only built on long time spent together while in the flesh. This is sureness of Oneness. Only time spent builds the steady time consuming required for Our love bond of Oneness. Spiritual Oneness is eternal, only time counts!

CONSTANT ATTENTION

It is step-by-step that I can draw you into your place with Me. Never let setbacks have unworthy setbacks. We are truly drawing together in ways meaningful to Me. This is your reward for work well done. It is constant attention and obedience that any real everlasting time comes about. Never think man's ways are the walk to be sought after for there is only non-worthwhile ongoing that way. It is only as I Lead that your path becomes fruitful. Keep drawing closer by time given to Me Just know this, *"Time is growing shorter and more precious"* **all of the time**. You cannot stretch time out, slow it down or speed it up. I control time and We only are to work time together to Our benefit. Learn this that I am speaking of and you will have made a giant leap upward!

A CALL

There is a call from Me buried in the heart of each child of Mine No one is born that I do not know. Can you see the true tragedy of the loss of each child of Mine? My dear ones pray for the lost children that can still be saved. "Yes. Lord! I pray now for all your lost children that can still be saved to seek truth now," make that your daily prayer My dear ones. Stir and awaken them dear Father to seek for their Father, and in truth asking for Jesus in truth!" **Let all your work now be wrapped up in this truth!** All the time now will never be enough. There is no loss to Me greater than this, but free will has a price I must pay! Perfection comes at such a dear cost! The salvation of the least one is a great event to Me. Can you see now why I say all are My Bride?

REALITY WALK

Make each day dawning a new walk beginning for you. Only by looking back will enlightenment beam forth. Reality brings a newness like never before and truth finds light casting no shadows. Watch carefully the walk of reality exposed. See into happenings with greater depth of perception. Be open to new areas of observance with new insight. Watch over new breaking situations as I give you guidance and foresight. Here is a word of notification requiring great thought, wisdom, and understanding. Ask the Father to help you to receive, understand, and then knowing do!

BE ONE

Each attempt, each try, and every outreach is well noted. Never fail by always trying. Progress with Me is the reaching Out with true desire. Results come to Me in Spirit, there is no better way! I see every effort and no effort fails! Only not trying is failure! Remember: I see the heart, and therein lay truth I bring. All truth originates with Me. No truth springs from nowhere, I am truth's only source. Seek truth find Me! Just know if I am not near you, you aren't anywhere! Don't seek Me any place because I Am. Where I am you are also! We are One when you just know! Seek to know! This opens wisdom beyond measure! We should not be close, but ONE! Don't just draw near Me, and let us Be ONE!

DAY BY DAY

Day-by-day I am with you, but are you with Me? I mean, We are close, but are We One? Only when you know, will you really know? Knowing is far above believing, knowing is well but there is still more, living as fully Mine is a step beyond. He who is a step beyond is far, far away from just knowing! These steps I here speak of are looking ahead toward man's ever growing walk. Some just receive and stay, Others walk a little, some seek and climb a bit, but I look for those who face the mountains and cliffs of difficulties with on-going and are unstoppable! When such are climbing they don't look for hand holds on the climb but seek My hand to hold! No one can climb by themselves to the place I am. Forget self, know only Me, and then your climb is level and smooth.

ONENESS COMING

This is Our walk, *"To be together always enjoying the Father and all of His Ways."* Know this is the time of change of eternity when your life is lost and His life becomes your on-going! These are then the days of forever on-going unfolding in His newness. You are One in His on-going and there is no more change, for One and always just are! To be seated at My right hand always is a fact existing first in My heart. It is then a forever truth that carries you anywhere, anytime, into My all only as I desire. Life eternal just is, for time has no meaning. It is just as desire unfolds to unravel events of My interest. Seated at My right hand is but an expression not explained with words, it is Spirit life. Always I have opened up these pictures as an opening into Our Oneness coming!

WHO WILL LISTEN?

Great is the Lord and greatly to be praised. This is as always should be, and is in your heart now because Our Oneness just is! Keep this word alive for truth walks in Oneness with all of My children. Who is Mine but those I have called, and who has answered readily but *those who hear!* Listen My dear ones for truth I give as ears are opened to hear. Listen, My children for how else will you know? By hearing Me you are drawn out of the world of the lost into My heart where you came from. All are called but all will not listen. How else will My children know? How often do I call, more than enough? Who will listen? Few, very few. Who will believe, only those who hear believing, then doing! I Call to the hearers and then the doers do! Listen My children in your hearts then instruct your heads to follow and do. Only by true doing will I know you who truly are called. I know who I call, but only can I tell they hear, who hear, by what they obey and do!

MY ONENESS

Our time builds, Our time grows, Our time carries My dreams, hopes, and all My desires, for Our time will never fail! Where there is no loss there is everlasting. Where perpetual growth is I am! Come My dear ones and abide in My forever as One with Me! Only Our walk, only Our time, only Our purpose will last and never fail. Listen, hear, grow close and know! All My children build and sow; this is My way they grow. Only wisdom with Spirit life knows! Keep open to hear, and listen is the way all truth comes day by day. Not by wishes, not by hopes, but by My Spirit knowing grows. Never forsake My stillness, for in there things find their existence! Dreams become desires that transpires. In My Oneness is My all, all of the time! Come into My Oneness and just BE!

TIMES OF TRUTH

Yes, these are times of great turmoil just ahead and nations will be tested and tried, and in the end all will know the hand of the Lord leads and guides Israel. The stage is about set and the release is about to be given when all My children will see the Lord because they will be like Him! Time is truly short! Gather together My dear ones knowing the time is upon you. Save the lost, gather in love dear ones, for I am your Savior and for these times the world has prepared. These are times for truth only truth for nothing else can open eyes of those to see. To see and know will bring all to their own tables to be served the dishes they have set for themselves by their own actions. I have called, and those who have ears to hear with hearts that respond to truth, will have picked the fruit on their plates!

LIFE WALKS

It is as each day is used that I find My dear ones, in the daily walk each child of Mine is exposed to this life, that he makes his place with Me or without Me. It is **in the walk** that I find the useful ones. I do not make My dear ones what they become, that is the purpose of each day they live. Wake up to this important word today for **this is the path of free will's desire** unfolding. Only as the life is lived will each of Us know the unveiling taking place. Life's walks become eternities plan unfolding for each one. Life eternal is the reward both for Us and for each one that comes with something to give to God's unfolding. Yes, each life has the opportunity to carry the love of God into his future desire. All life surviving is God's love seeking enriching by expanding. All eternity is just love unfolding in greater and greater expression. All life unfolding is God's love making His expressions show more and more. All of these words given are but fodder for growing new expressions in love! Lives lost are only useless fodder of lost endeavors. Nothing God does is without its purpose!

TRUTH LIFTS UP

All that I speak, I give freely to all that have ears to hear. But proper hearing requires proper doing, this also I require of man. Those who hear Me properly are to be burdened with the task of doing! This doing is to the credit of all works. I require that all should hear, but not all should do. For freely I give, that from My giving some should live. All do not live from all I give, for it is only as their doing pleases Me can man rise up to live. All lives are precious to Me but not to man. It is the wisdom of man seeking truth that truth lifts him up to live. Those wise in their heart will know Me from their start. All who I call are not hearers of My heart. The man who hears must also hear rightly! This means only truth springs from those to who truth is real. Truth that is real brings honor men feel. Blessed are all truth seekers who hearing do! Oh, Lord your words of protection seem endless in their perfection!

WORDS OF BLESSING

Yes, I bring to you My words of blessing to My children who I Love. By words do I lead, by words do I direct, by words do I channel blessings of great worth to all who hear, believe, and do! Is it not reasonable these things I here have said? All things exist because of My words and surely they are worthy now! Give long, and on-going, yes intent thought to these words here written, for by My words I speak, "worlds are created!" Man is no little thing to Me, all men are from Me, but not all men come to Me, yet all men are forever! It is men who I give power of choice and many fail for their selfish flaws flourish because of free-will! Free will is the great separator I use to bring selection to perfection. As cream rises to the top so will the cream of My creation come to My perfection! It is not with careless thought I created man in Our image. The children of worth will walk as the image of My pattern forever, for they are Myself, love, expanded!

BY MY WORDS

Words, words, words, are they not the building blocks of heaven? Have I not said by My words I have formed man in Our image? All of creation has come forth as I have spoken. See that you know in your heart these things I say, for as I speak you have life forever more. Only by My words can you live and have your existence! Yes, as truth flows by My words it is only in this action can believing behold creation in truth! For only in truth does My creation grow into your place of forever with Me. My words carry the weight of My purpose into realms of forever. It is in this manner all of My children will come into the reality of all of the word places I bring forth. So I now caution you, watch the words of your mouth for as I Am so will you be.

NO ONE WAY!

When you are teaching, and you make listening the goal, then should follow the lessons with instructions in getting wisdom! So as you are doing, you do so as I desire! Be blessed by these instructions for they are true, honest, and good! You should then thank the Lord that you are able to make truth come out plain and true. Only by following My instructions can any child of Mine learn the true path I set for them. It is foolish for everyone to be given the same message over and over again when so many children need their individual path to pursue. This is the ***great necessity***, **all shall be taught of the Lord!** In this manner, I am more able to draw each one into their individual path that I have set for them to reach their highest and best place with Me!

Shouldn't this be also made clearer to each dear one I seek? And I ask, "Why these desires of Mine aren't made more clear to My children? Only because through their "denominations" men have tried to separate for themselves what they think best for man. Many have chosen some worthwhile methods of Mine but all have missed My heart's desire! Bring each dear one to Me, and I will teach them the way they should go. There is no "one way" for all of My children have their differences that please Me! (John 6:45)

INTO HIS PRESENCE

As the calendar marks the days, so do I count and watch over these days just ahead. Days of culmination, days of final gathering, Yes, days of great climax! The Father has **THE DAY** built in His heart and no man knows, but he has shown the worthy ones the way is building to His great climax! He said My dear ones shall know the signs and the times, and that makes Me free to speak about this close coming wonder in the heavens! Nothing, no nothing before or after is going to make a mark in the heart of the Father that the day of the catching away of this part of His family will make. "All out," yes, He is going all out for this wonderful event! Yes, a great group of His beloved ones have been taken up before. But that was a more secret, silent, little spoken of or announced. Jesus' lifting all paradise, with Abraham's Bosom, with Him to heaven! This time is to bring all of His Bride from heaven and earth into His marvelous presence. I've given you in the past some pictures of this event, still the actual occasion will burst all bonds of telling!

OUR FATHER

Yes, it is in study of My words that heavenly wisdom will enter the hearts of My children. No other way works better than applying self to My ways. Each child of Mine, whether a Solomon or a farmer all are the same, they need (must have) wisdom as their companion. No one is exempt, no one is so special! It is in self-control that obedience will grow. All must by their free-will be taught by Me. Sooner or later, sooner is better! Your "heart attitude" for My way is the test of your worth to Me. I check true hearts! This that I bring to you, I will bring equally to all who willingly apply themselves to My plan for them. Only My plan for them counts. It is My forever you are invited into, and My plan and things that I freely offer. When you freely make Me your Father your way is *freely* set!

THE FAMILY

The words I have given are meant to be unfolded unto those to whom I draw before you. Make every effort to bring My teachings as I desire them to be given! I never waste My time or your time. When proper attention is given then proper blessings unfold. Seek to hear and to do the things unveiled, for in them and by them My work carries on. Attention to My plan brings Me closer and closer to your completion. Watch carefully over all I am releasing now, more than ever! Great and terrible tidings are coming, but My children shall only see or hear of them. All events must be released to bring proper conclusion to the things of the past already said. My plans are ever on-going to no known end! Where eternity is, are where We all have come from and where We all are going. The family of My heart was with Me from its start, and it will be so forever!

MY HAND

Try to think about My position of watching over all My dear ones, yes watching as they make errors, failures, blunders, and mistakes. The stories and tales are countless, but all those occasions are also true life! It is only the truth in each life that brings My truth into their reality. By the many odd or different situations life training is to be experienced. I'm not causing these situations, but I will try to use them as teaching tools. What is My point today? My dear ones use each experience as a means of learning something about others, you, or Me. Yes, look for My hand in daily activities, and I can use your experience to build and grow a better tomorrow!

LISTEN, HEAR, AND DO

It is in the doing each day I can direct your path. To the non-doers I have nothing for them. How can I bring worth when nothing is forthcoming to work with or for? All that I declare I will do, so should My children do. Am I not your guide, teacher, and helper? Why not? How can I guide, lead, direct, and or otherwise help those who won't or don't do? All is waiting, Yes, **all** is waiting for My children, who are listeners only, to become doers! Over and over, I call My dear ones, but do they answer? No, I hear no good word! Cooperation makes benefit apparent, but nothing is the display of hearers only. You say, but what can I do? Only what I ask of you, We must talk, you must learn to listen, and then obey. Great things are building a pile of nothing for no one to see when My dear ones never learn to listen, hear, and do!

BEYOND NOW

It is the works of My hands that My heart hungers for. Yes, I long to see the unfolding of My love in the works of My dear Ones. Our true togetherness will show forth as My children in truth, faith, and obedience show forth the works, the desires of My heart. This then becomes the realm of Our forever showing forth the greatness and wonders of My creation's on-going into the great realms yet unseen and unknown! The eternity that I take My children into has vast greatness and wonders far beyond your words can know expression. I only say these things now because I want your dreams and hope to have a foundation to build upon in this part of now! Yes, your dreams, hopes, and fancy desires are only to be a start of Our wonderful walk of forever! You now know nothing about Our "Sea of Nothing" to unfold throughout eternity! Yes, far past the visible universe you now see, is merely a peek of My now behind the curtain of cosmic darkness!

ALLNESS

In this work you are now engaged in (reading) flows only words, but be wise, it is by My words all is created! As My words become the words and way of all of My children then will the vast occasions of the future come into their separate activity? This that I now am speaking about is where the flow of all future will exist. All future is only My presence expanding! Our growing Oneness has the ability to draw all past and future into Our walk of Oneness. This is a statement of truth requiring your understanding for all of My family must come into My reality at sometime! I bring this idea up now because I desire truth to prevail! This is to grow in importance as We walk together, how can My children be like Me if they are never exposed slowly to this ALLNESS of which I'm now speaking?

TRUTH EVERMORE

It is in this work We are doing that I can lay before the readers of worth truth forevermore. Keep always in your heart this hunger for truth! Only by and through truth can anything of Mine have true existence; untruth, and falseness, diminishes and disappears. Only truth floats in life! truth is the beautiful carrier of desires exposed. No other source will find life forevermore. This new realm of forever I'm opening is the endless chambers of My hopes and dreams. Reality is only as I release the on-going of events planned in My hopes and desires. In all of the tomorrows for My children will be found the truths of My children's dreams, hopes, and desires. When My Oneness is filled with My children then will Our Oneness find truth forevermore!

LOVE GROWING

All the works of man that I allow of Him are only to fill his needs until he finds Me. Then, My dear ones, that man should turn from serving himself and those around him and serve Me! This then is the path most fruitful for him. However I leave all this in

His hands. I will make no man be obedient unto Me. It is love growing love that I wait upon, for only love draws the worthy ones! This is My love sown in the secret heart of every man. A flesh walk of worth is a flesh walk that knows of Me in their heart and if it doesn't seek Me on its own at least is awakened when I pass by seeking them! The ones I seek are those who are stirred in their hearts when I pass by. Look for My dear ones; yes, seek for these children I desire as if they were silver and gold for your treasure, for they are all of that for My treasure!

TRUTH FLOWS

Our walk carries many blessings for many children of worth to Me. By My words I teach, lead, guide, and bless all those with listening ears and hearts of obedience! Truth flows freely to all who will give time to believing in Truth. I am truth and by My words I build, create, lead, and bless My dear ones who are attentive to the things of My heart. Only hearing ones can be taught properly, this is by My Spirit indwelling them. I said it is better that I go, for then I could send to the obedient ones the Holy Spirit. He is the source of all blessings for

My dear ones. Only by your obedience can the gift given be unwrapped. Yes, a gift of on-going evidence to all who are attentive and receptive. Learn to listen in your heart for I am with you through it all always.

STUDY MY WORD

It is in your hourly study of My Word that your daily walk will be a blessing to Me, and then also to My children around you. Do not disregard the worth of your study of My word, not just to your own way, but give proper consideration to the benefits it may bring to others around you. In each life that comes to Me I must find the worth of it exhibited in some manner to others. How else will the lost ever find truth unless I have truth carriers do their work I give them? Proper growth of truth throughout the world will only come as My truth is shared with My true truth carriers! Give more than just a passing thought to all this here given today. It is day-by-day in obedience to the things I say, or have said, that the worthwhile exhibit of My truths is displayed! Be a showcase of the beauty of truth that I have given to you, and you will find the beauty I desire you to have!

WALK I DESIRE

As your fingers carry a pen across the pages before you I release truth from My heart to be carried into My loved ones hearts. Record all this that I desire to say for it is by My words I am building truth that flows lifting My dear ones into realms of truth for their enlightenment. Only by recording My truths day-by-day can I show My Love unfolding in a manner pleasing to Me! This is daily showing building blocks of truth that opens doors of blessings. Only by the on shinning of My truths can I keep spreading the healing salve of love through words. It is by My words planted I can grow My love Bride. Come dear reader of these truths flowing and enlarge your understanding in the ways that teach. This is an end time blessing, teaching the walk I desire each to have. Spiritual growth comes truly from My hand of guidance only! Oh, you dear seekers know truth and see!

ONENESS BE

It is slowly, without haste, I build My kingdom, and that which becomes My kingdom will grow on into My forever. World without end in which all My men blend. As I am complete in Myself, so I will make all men complete in Me. When My Son and I hold out the kingdom to men to occupy We are also holding out Our own selves for all to be as We are. Have I not said "Are ye not God's? Yes, dear ones I say listen with your ears to truth said, but you must hear My truth alive in your own heart. I do not carelessly say to man, "are ye not Gods"? For how else can My kingdom reign unless My kingdom is all of Me and My likeness? As I am so shall all of My kingdom be. Children, you are to be children no more, but all shall know Me as One. What else should Oneness be unless it is as I say? *Psalm 82:6, and John 10:34 both agree about Ye are Gods. John 5:18; Jesus equal to God. John 17:21; All men be one.*

CONFIDENCE

It is with confidence every child of Mine believes I know him and love him, and that I have called him. This walk in confidence believing is the only way to come along and keep Me by your side. If one doubts, questions, and is always seeking and asking why, will he ever come to the conviction I require that is just knowing? Our walk will never occur without the knowing in your heart you are Mine and I am yours! This belief is the mark of truth I look for. Only when questioning doubts about Our relationship is put away can Our true walk begin. Do you begin understand? How can I relate heavenly truths to anyone who isn't sure what Our relationship is? True believers then are also identified by their truth seeking! Who can climb a ladder unless they know what it is leaning on, and where they are going? Make your ladder lean on truth, and just know I am holding it safely for you! You've all heard about climbing "The ladder of success" but which of you have ever asked what it is leaning on?

TRUTH TO HEAR

Day-by-day I give forth truth for My children to hear, but how many are there who ***truly listen in their hearts***? I admonish all who have the capability to "listen and hear." ***Yes, this is the walk in the Spirit I give that all My children live the life I willingly set before them.*** How can you My dear ones not listen and hear as I desire them to do? Why must I repeat over and over the true path of the Spirit of light and Life?

Listen and hear in your heart the way I give you to freely come into My heart to dwell forever! Caution is well and good, but only when it is protecting you from evil, but where caution is not properly applied, it restrains and stops your progress I would have you attain. Until My dear ones are freely open to and accepting this path of Spirit growth where are they?

SEEK AND KNOW

It is as I require, all men to seek and know Me! However so few ever even barely attempt to do so! It is through My personally speaking to those who do listen for Me that I find pleasure in closely working daily with any and all who willingly give Me their time? Why is it so few will willingly open up themselves to walk and talk daily with Me? It is from men, through evil activities from their hearts, that others have picked up a promoted the lies and dangers of delving into "Spiritual ways." These stories of course had much truth to promote because of Satan's activities. But why My children who read the Bible so carry Satan's words of fear in their hearts that they won't come readily to Me in the Spirit? *This should not be*! How many times in My Word have I said, "fear not?" Over and over again, yet My dear ones are so hesitant to draw as close as I desire. Teach truth, spread truth, and draw all who will be obedient in their hearts to My will and way. The time now is the last of these great times of obeying!

THE GOAL

It is with pleasure I bring you words for My children, and it will be to your credit when truth is read and acted upon bringing My truths into action. My plans speak and live in truth, and in and by truth all things come about as I desire. No walk is perfect for man, but every obedient walk becomes perfection in My plan! I know the way, and My way is far above man's plans. Keep My goal as your goal and you'll find My perfection showing at Our completion! No work I start is lost for all have My foundation to build on. Keep My goal ever before you, then your path will be without hindrances. As We build together you grow! To be My companion is to walk streets of gold that We own! Always keep open to My voice, knowing I know where We are going. No man knows the end until We get there, so enjoy the walk each moment on the way. The days just ahead have wonders unfolding better left unsaid. Never be in confusion for I know conclusions, are you not in My hands forever?

TRUE PROCESS

If My children would diligently process My Word, they could find I have released truth sufficient to draw them into My saving truth. But finding "saving truth" is not the goal to stop at, for it is **but their first step to take.** It will then be up to them to find Me in their heart where I then will lead and guide them into Our Oneness! This is My true process of all everlasting worth to be given to each one of My children. I Love all equally, but all do not respond sufficiently to come to Me in their ultimate Oneness of all worth! This process of gaining love in truth is an everlasting walk. To become fully as I am will never be the goal reached but the true goal of My children is to be "in" My image and likeness. Sufficient is the place of forever to fulfill each and everyone's heart to a richness of endless overflowing!

GROWING ONENESS

It is from the heart of man I see the what, and where he Is. I see into his very self, the one in which My Holy Spirit lives. Here is truth of his heavenly birth, and so I know in whom he lives and breathes! We are growing in Our Oneness, and it is here We now live and have Our growing Oneness. Yes, the crux of all true walking is found where day-by-day Our togetherness grows. Never doubt, never think or imagine a turning away, for here is the forever of Our love growing! Keep this place of "growing knowing" expanding and holding tighter and tighter this that We are sharing more and more. Yes, here is the preciousness that I give reference to in the Bible! Here is the seat of your walk of forever where love is hatched into an ever growing miracle I watch and cherish. Here lies the private annex to the fellowship hall of Our forever! Proverbs 20:15.

TESTED AND TRIED

The days of man should grow in preciousness as he draws closer to My truths in his amazement! All My truths should be his first and most important desires. This then should become his goal of forever, "To know Me more and more." **Only** by gaining **This knowing** will any man ever be pleasing to Me as he should! I am easily pleased by men who wake up to the reality of Me, and My works. There are special children that I watch over. I watch a long time over each one because I'm testing and trying all men for their possible usefulness to My kingdom. Yes, I do not hastily choose anyone. You would be greatly surprised at the time I take sometimes. It is in this deliberation that proper selection can be made. Only true hearts forever are what are desired. The carefree selection is forever protection, false entries are not welcome. Be comforted by this reality of truth, it is for eternities protection that I make careful selection!

THE REALITY

The reality of truth should awaken man to My deeper things of the Spirit, for only "in the Spirit" does My true guidance come. Hear well what is here said, for these words are My deep Spiritual truths, **The walk I call all men to come to.** Why do I take so long watching each child of Mine! Because of the ultimate "preciousness" of love forever. Never miss or overlook where this walk of man in the Spirit leads him. My goal I've never hidden, I have plainly said I make man in My Spirit, and in My likeness and My image! What can that be except, "I make man a God." Truth I give, but the ultimate place and goal THE TRUE FOREVER WALK OF MAN I HAVE NEVER TOLD ANYONE! This today is a thought provoker; use it to great advantage by sitting with Me in silence and in truth where I live forever. Didn't I say worship Me in Spirit and in truth. John 4:22,23.

LEAST OR MOST

With daily attention given unto the things I desire then a man shall begin to know Me. But for Me to know a man I take his whole lifetime into consideration. Yes, I watch over all men all of the time. Are they not all from My desire? It is by My careful attention and watch over each one I can find those that truly will be My worthy ones of perfection. No, I do not choose My dear ones easily, I wait to give them full opportunity to show and display their possible worth! It is by My careful watch that slowly I decide who will be most and who will be least in My heavens! Each one is given full time to grow and show Me where their heart will be. Many are lost and many are found at the moment I choose! I seek loving hearts and loving ways. I seek "the seeking ones." Yes, seek Me with your whole heart and you will be precious in My kingdom. The flesh time is the choosing time; there is no other time to be given!

ACTION IN TRUTH

Daily this walk reveals My love and desires. Daily do I seek children who read, and knowing truth, they are told to obey. How else can I make meaningful choices if My dear ones only sit and stay where I found them? Action in truth displayed is My way of choosing My worthy ones! Have I not made it clear enough in My Holy Bible by stories and testimonies how I expect you to walk and grow closer to Me? Where have I failed you? No you fail Me when your path is made plain before you, but you stir not! Daily is the walk I require in obedience to what I have already written in My Holy Bible. But there is more I have asked, "Hear Me in your heart daily." Have I not said enough? Many think they listen, but do they hear rightly and obey?

TO BE ONE

This on and on of My words is an endless flow to My children. It is My most important task in forever! Yes, get used to hearing My words flowing in your heart, for only in Our oneness can such a gift be perfectly understood. Hear now truth that is bound to you forever! My dear ones only your walk with Me leading and guiding will you ever be! This is your safety net to dwell in; this is your hope of glory forevermore. "We are to be One" has this truth ever been made clear enough that your response should be a "Thank you ringing out forever? Come and respond now in such truth that you'll be forever before Us, together.

OUR WALK DESIRED

When My words dwindle and fail then should your course be altered, for this is a sign of failing in your life! Only together in truth forever will you grow closer to Me all of the time. Never fail to pay attention to My words. Past, present, and future are built into life forevermore with the guidance of My words flowing. Truth leads, truth guides, truth's walk is one sure path, never falter, never waver, and you'll never fail! To grow closer with Me is to continually increase into your place of wonderful truth. This walk is **the only way** of My satisfaction being perfected. Our walk is the forever way of victory desired unfolding. Where you are to go, how you are to go, why your are to go only unfolds as Our closeness grows. Make truth seeking love's walk of forever and I will increase Our Oneness! I never fail to support a true truth seeker's walk of purity! Make your walk one of Our togetherness growing!

HEART TALK

Read and reread My words for I do not give anyone instant revelation of all I mean when I speak in their heart. My words carry revelation far beyond what is merely heard the first time! Heed this Word and give thought to it today and in coming days. Meditation brings compensation. Keep always open for more and more. I do not speak with haste; My words never carry a bad taste! To ponder and dwell in the thoughts I bring by words of truth, will open treasures to many things! Words, My words, live and are ever living ringing out across the universe. Give deep, long thought to what is here written for much wealth is buried in what has just been written!

THIS TIME NOW

As you have seen in My Word. the Holy Bible, how I kept good watch over My children of Jerusalem at times, and times all of My choosing, so do I keep watch over all of My children, especially in this now time of completion, for My children of the gentiles. Yes, this time now, just before Jacob's time of the completion, is a time most cherished by Me. This too is a time of gathering that touches My heart. These are days of wrap-up for an age long looked for and needed in the purpose of My eternal plan. Every child gathered is a treasure for Me, and My purpose is to come to its perfect completion. Hear this word today in your heart, each one who I gather to read of this My desire for the now of My time!

REVELATION GROWS

With careful searching Our past records you will find new treasures to behold. As I have said, My revelation knowledge keeps on giving when compatible hearts seek! It is not necessary for all to be revealed at once when the revelation keeps on opening up! Slow going proves safe ongoing. Haste builds waste! With considered care with the things I share I will bring safely all without despair. Our agreement only builds slowly for My truths cover time unknown, and are only slowly shown. When I am the inevitable what is the hurry? Won't I always be before you, behind you, and right inside you? I am the All knowing one, you are the growing one!

ONLY BY OBEDIENCE

Our walk together only grows when in togetherness We move. Only by your obedience to My Spirit within you, only by obedience to My Word, only in obedience to your own will and way, and only in Our togetherness can you progress. I do not intend to tell you what to do step by step, haven't you noticed this by now? Our walk only becomes "Our walk" when you just move as if We both were in agreement. This also becomes My way of testing you! You must gain a true freedom walk in all We do together. You will grow into knowing that which I am saying. You are to freely, "act like I am leading you freely" through your heart of free obedience. Don't you comprehend this meaning of Oneness? Oneness is you moving as I desire because I inspire you to do what I require. I am not your dictator telling you what to do. Now do you more clearly see this direction We are going?

TREASURE BURIED

It is with no regrets that I pursue each one I call to bring more and more of the treasure buried. Yes, I have hidden many great treasures in the precious ones I have called. It is through time spent growing into the Spirit I have called forth that My truths and wonders are to be revealed. Only I see and know the things of worth each called one should show. Have great patience with one another for you know not who are those I here speak of! Many are called, but few seem ready to answer that call I buried. It is with great patience that I too must wait, sadly some never seem to respond, and gifts are lost and buried! Be not like one who is blessed but never allows the gift given to unfold. Most of My work is never revealed, but some still blossom forth and My wonders are displayed bringing great blessings and opportunity by seeking and believing that there dwells in you a gift yet to be exposed!

SHORT TIME LEFT

When We sit together each morning never let a gift go to waste by lack of attention! Keep always open for this sharing of Our words is a mighty revelation that has unfolding worth that will keep on giving over and over again! It is with deliberate concern that I say this now because of Our short time left! My words are ones of construction, this is their purpose I send them forth, therefore to slow down, block, or stop them will cause many lessons of great worth to be lost! This is a flow of blessings like a steam of water, did it not say in Jer. 2:13 *"For My people have committed two evils; they have forsaken Me the fountain of living waters, and hewed them out cisterns, broken cisterns, that can hold no water."* These things today I have written as a warning both to the writer and the reader of My words. Give attention to only My things now, My dear children!

KEEP ON SEEKING

My breakthroughs come only to My children who will seek and keep on seeking! This My children is the blessing of Abraham flowing as Jesus promised in Galatians 3:5-9; so all should believe in and adhere to and trust in and rely on the message that here is written. Give deeper thought about these written words I have put before you so often, yet you do not seek the Spiritual truth hidden, but only go by what you have been taught by man teaching My Word. Is it not clear that behind many of My written words I have kept the Spiritual meanings hidden until the seeking hearts go after the buried Spiritual truths of My heart? This opening of the "revelation knowledge" in My written Scriptures are used to teach the children who seek to draw closer and closer for more and more of My truth.

FILLED WITH TRUTH

As I pour forth these words of great encouragement I find too the joy of the release of truth. Everlasting truth is free and open to all those I love, and it is My pleasure to release truth to water pots that seek filling. Few are there who openly look for the place where truth resides forever, believing it is available to them also who love and seek the path of truth forevermore. Yes, all My dear ones will be filled when truth seeking is their purpose. When the Bible says "I am truth" (about Jesus) then know that is a blessing for all My children, have I not said you are to be like Jesus? All My sons and daughters are of truth, and all shall be as I Am! *Pay attention*, I have never said just when! Truth flowing is ever on-going with the end "*A certain place forever*!

HEAR IN YOUR HEART

Of all the ways I communicate with Man the one I've chosen for My loved Ones **is for them to hear Me in their heart.** This truly indicates the closeness of love that I can work with. To teach this in truth is the way for Me to bring all those who will grow closer in all I desire to do in Our forever. This gift must flow while they are in the flesh for then I can more easily see those whose hearts are right with Me. Here is My selection made easy without prejudice! For true love to grow it must expose its self in and obvious manner. **This is the real beginning for the secrets of My plan to**

flow into vessels of worth for the proper unfolding of eternity! Yes, seek to teach a way for more and more of My children to wake up to the true path to and through My heart!

HEART GROWTH

There is never a right time for My children to grow or to choose their way with Me. For only when their desire meets My desire will release be given. I am waiting and looking for heart growth, and your heart growth is waiting for action! Only by your action seeking Me with purpose to pursue only My way for you will We ever come to Our right time! It isn't the time that's right; it's just your heart! Now hear this Word in your heart, for I am always ready, waiting, and willing for your action to become Our action!

Your only worthwhile growth is when I am leading you, so guess how that works, "Only when you grow by listening to My words of growth for you!" Have I not said the same thing you should do over and over again? Read Rev. 2:7, 11, 17, 29; and Rev. 3:6, 13, 22.

GROW DAILY

It is My desire for My chosen ones to grow daily into My plan for them. Why daily? Think about it, don't I have a lot to say to those who are to be made fit to be called My chosen ones? Am I not displaying each morning now the extent and size of all I have to say? Doesn't it seem right to give Me all of your time now, when you look back on the time that has passed already? Yes, dear ones, when I say I want all of your time now **it is only for your benefit!** Don't you yet realize how much I have to teach you to bring you into the place of My desire for you? When will those "saved ones" wake up to the absolute greatness of wonder of their salvation, and ever ongoing wealth of their walk with Me? Our time together is to be ever-expanding, ever growing, and ever increasing in value to Me, and to each ones precious walk! You, each one, are to leave your earth place of little worth to My places for you of ever increasing wealth! You should be more eager to draw closer to Me when you view the Heavens above that I am calling you to!

HEAR AND RECORD

As we come together each morning, there builds a connection of great worth to Me, and worth to come to you. I am slow to move when the permanence is a forever thing, so only in patience will My blessings unfold. This too is a test of deciding! My children's walk with Me; all take a personal turn when they listen to My words for them each morning. How else can I personally bring true guidance for each one if I can't personally have time and their attention to do so?

Hear and record these words I bring. This will have a two-fold purpose! One is the setting of the listener's place with Me, and the other is to set his work I require of him! All My children of worth will have this part to obey. How else can My work through them be effective? I bring these simple truths now to plainly show I have a workable method that is simple for any child in the flesh. But who is there that will listen, hear, and obey?

A WORD DOER

It is not *"the when"* you'll do something for Me it is *"the if"* you'll do something for Me that must be made clear between Us! You are My friend when you prove you'll obey and do things I ask. Our growing together is all about you. If you'll obey? If you'll do? And if you'll do, just when you will do? You see, I will be very slow in drawing you close, it will take time, testing, errors, corrections, etc. Is this Our walk truly a walk together? When will it be a walk where I am always the leader? When will these questions be important enough that you will seek Me and spend time with Me and learn to **know** Me and all I have for you? In other words when will you sit with Me every morning and pay attention to the things I tell you, so you will truly become a doer of the word.

THE WHOLE WALK

Your walk with Me is a walk in the flesh while growing in the Spirit. Our walk becomes a walk of proper purpose when you assume all aspects of it as they come, knowing We are in this together. Ups and downs are the life of the flesh, how else can testing and trials be made meaningful? Only the whole walk, the whole way counts. Keep only the final goal in sight, for these times are fast diminishing to vanish forever!

ROAD TO WALK

These times are changing man for better or for worst. Separation is coming among My children even they are sensing the change. Some even will fall away from Me in self-pleasing and ease when these times call for witnessing and action! Come and awaken the tired and weary to rise again and pay attention to Me and My ways. Only constant striving will prove your place with Me. Seek after more and more of My ways for you. My children have not yet struggled as they should. These are due times of testing and teaching that draws all closer to Me when they listen for My call in their hearts. Wake up to these times for I have still much to do. **The path of truth seeking is the only road to walk on to daily improve your way with Me!**

LET VICTORY RING

It is better to do a little than nothing. To do a little however, lacks the obedience that doing much takes for true victory to show with the glory that God the Father has waiting for all who march to obedience's music! The true sound of victory rings so loud many hearts are stirred by its compelling sound. The best of a victory's sound brings hearts to attention, and stirs many to strive to greater heights! All striving has in it the ingredients of a worthy life lived for others, as well as self! Self's death in victory is the joy to be sought with all of one's strength and all of one's heart, for through the heart's struggle grows God's children of great worth!

WORD MOST PRECIOUS

This slow unfolding of the truths of God that is being brought forth daily through the written words given to you is to prove of great worth to the children unto whom true truth is waved as their banner of forever! **No other recording such as this is set anywhere else.** Keeps this word of truth flowing as long as I give it to you, for this is and has been My will to be done! Precious are My words so give them more attention more of the time. The great task to be accomplished has never been made clear; but now is plainly said what is the source and purpose of all that has already been done. There is more and more to come until I say enough!

TRUE TRUTH IS HERE WAVED AS THE CHILDREN'S BANNER OF FOREVER

TRUTH RULES

It is the day-by-day persistence in truth that gives Me the right of ownership over all that truth proclaims. Yes, it is truth that confers My ownership of all I create or desire. Only truth rules as the victor over all doers! Make truth and the pursuit of truth the foremost of any activity in which you participate, for truth is of Me and I watch carefully over all truth bringing it all under My watchful eye. My children are called to truth, only truth, for it is the certificate of entry into My kingdom! Jesus is My Son of truth as are all who I give entry into My kingdom. A truth carrier has all My protection over them for all time in My everywhere! How is this to be so you ask? Am I not present in the heart of everyone who is or ever to be? Be careful of all who are Mine, for am I not present in them always? Can you not yet see how all of this that I here say is only the making of Oneness of which I indwell

HEART'S CRY

It is in this continual seeking for the truth of God, that God gives release to truth! Yes, truth seeking builds sanctuaries of truth places where true hearts find peace, comfort, and Spiritual growth from Father God Himself. ***Let every soul be subject unto the Higher Powers, for there is no power but of God: the powers that be are ordained of God***! Romans 13:1, 2. *"Let every soul be subject unto the higher powers. For there is no power but of God: the powers that be are ordained of God. Whosoever therefore resisteth the power, resisteth the ordinance of God: and they that resist shall receive unto themselves damnation!"* This is not anything but submission unto the love that covers all who are ordained of God in love of truth! It is the seeking that comes from the cry of the heart that finds fulfillment in the drawing closer and closer to the Oneness that draws!

ONLY SEEKERS

There are secrets of life and secrets of eternity that I have held because My richness I do not readily display before everyone. Only the seekers of truth, who I come to trust, will ever find My nuggets of truth that amaze and appeal to the open hearts of tomorrow. When My true truth flows it will not be open to the world of flesh like I will open it to those of eternity. All who are invited into My eternity are not privileged to see, know, or experience the all of My everything. Kingdoms are for all, but all of My Kingdom is not for all of the members. Just as earth's kingdoms have places of greater and greater privilege so does My Kingdom of forever. The King still has His privileges of places and positions! As I have revealed little about My Sea of Nothing I have also indicated that is My Place of special privilege. The kingdoms of the earth of the past are only minor representatives of My Kingdoms of the earth and My Kingdoms of the universe to be! There is one thing that is universal and of forever that is My Love!

EARTH

As I preserve My loved ones I also preserve all that I hold dear. The earth is a special place, My womb of heaven. In it I have ordained that I shall inherit My family of My universe. It shall be for Me, My watched over place of great worth; when I planned My heavens to be, I set them apart to appear in the sequence of My timing. I spread out the pleasures of forever that My children shall have time to participate, and find pleasure in all the works of My hands. This that I speak of now is the simple picture that is to unfold into the forever of My heavenly places. I will leave no stone unturned so every child of Mine shall find their places of great worth displayed in the beauty and wonderment of My desire for them.

THIS WALK

Our walk has taken many a strange turn when viewed from man's position, but what man can see Our true place or position? It is this growing walk and way that all of My children must take. This walk is strange only to the unbelievers view, but where do they stand when they try to see Us? **Seek more and more to hear your truth from My voice in your heart!** This is the walk of preciousness I desire for every child of Mine. How few truly walk this walk of love in trust and believing? The ones who seek in the flesh never know or truly see just what he is becoming or just how it is coming about! All this is growth in the Spirit while captured in the flesh! Have courage, and trust in this walk for every child must seek it, and find it to be pleasing to Me!

THANKSGIVING

Yes, make this day a day of thanksgiving for so few of My children truly see all their blessings that I lay before their feet. Stir up the Spirit within each child of Mine that I may know their love is real! As rejoicing touches your hearts know that My heart is pleased! Keep this Spirit of family and oneness growing for that truly is My Spirit with you! Let this growing evidence of the truth of Our growing oneness become evident to this world of trials and troubles, for mankind is digging a pit of evil for their own purposes. My children must be My witnesses of truth for this time is one of trials, troubles and separation from the plan of salvation I have desired for all men.

THE KNOWING

Only slowly and with deliberateness will My children learn to come to Me in Spirit and in truth! Truth is the great separator that all My children must come to know and be a part of. Only by this very deliberate move will any child come into "The knowing" that makes them Mine forever! I am not hasty in making My choice of children; this is a blessing to all because when the choice is made neither of Us can change ways after that! Once and for always you become My dear family! This is My most sought desire! Make it yours also! eternal oneness, which I have spoken of often, is the aim of all Our work throughout the ages past, with still a short while to wrap up the loose ends, then the truth exposed envelopes all with its wrapping of Love!

TOGETHERNESS

It is the slow unfolding of My family plans that keeps everything moving in their proper order. Nothing I have done or am doing or will be doing is done in haste. This is part of My careful watch over all My children's ways to be. You also should learn to be deliberate in all you do. It is this care in action that I can help control to keep your way safe and sure. Your hasty moves become all yours, for I will back away to see just what you are pursuing. You see all your moves should be done together with Me, how else can I be partner with you if We don't talk it over and make Our plans together? Togetherness is the lesson most desired. Seek this togetherness for it is slippery as an eel!

MOST DESIRED

This day-by-day talk is where Spirit growth brings truth plainly shown. What use is truth but to show My way to the lost. Keep always before you this carrying truth for the children. Always remember I am not bringing truth out to show to the world, but only truth out to My children in growth training! No true Spirit growth is ever attained unless Spirit growth is most desired! This desire building does not come to the flesh but to the Spirit of man only; therefore, spend more time thinking of this side of what is written. The eye of the flesh must give growth to the eye of the Spirit in man. Only as the Spirit of man attains to truth can truth release My love through this truth training! Steps to take first must be found, then believed, then acted upon by the flesh. Men still in the flesh are most desired by the Father when they awaken to this proper walk after the Spirit!

HEARING, YOU DO

Sometimes I give the same lesson over and over. Why, because the simplicity of all I have to say is to **"be just like Me."** Yes, did I not teach by action to reaction? My lessons were simple ones. Did I not say to My disciples leave clothes, money, your all, and go do the things you saw Me do? What do I say now to you? Go do as I would do! The learning lessons are those doing. How can you be like Me? Do as I was doing! Am I not with you in all things? Will I teach you differently than I taught Peter? No! Hear in your heart what I have to say to you. Just as you learn as you are reading, so do I desire to teach you as you listen and hearing you do! Yes, seek more and more by listening more and more! How else can I make you One with Us?

TRUE WORLD

Yes, all My children begin to be when they have the Holy Spirit, and they only grow as they take on more and more of the Spirit. Jesus comes into them, and then I come into them. No one ever comes into My place unless they are just like Me! My true world is the world of the Spirit where all truth dwells. My dear children wake up to this truth and eagerly seek to grow! Our walk is the walk of forever and always; but it is only for children who grow to be just like Me. In My image and in My likeness in all that they are. There is no other life eternal unless they are just like Me! This is the protection required to dwell where I dwell and live as I live. Why else would I go to all this effort to bring man along? This is the only way to eternity for My family!

CONNECT

Though I am too complex for mere man to really know, My children will know Me for they will all be just like Me. This dear ones is necessary for their eternal protection. My realms are made for Spirit dwelling and man must be like Me to be able to receive all that the Father desires for His family to have. Is it not made clear enough in My Bible? Yes, when properly read and believed. Many children need to read with comprehension, that is why they must be baptized into the Holy Spirit. **It is not enough to "have the Holy Spirit," but the Holy Spirit must be listened to and be obeyed!** This is missing in most churches, the importance of the Holy Spirit. How can I draw you into My

Kingdom when He who will bring you into My Kingdom is ignored? Yes, My children must be baptized into the Spirit and speak in other tongues, how else can they be taught Spirit things unless they connect with Me through the Holy Spirit?

MY WAY

The teaching of My children takes much time, thought, and effort and is My job to finish and make right. All We can do while you're in the flesh is use the Bible to turn hearts until they will willingly come to Me every morning and be taught their personal lessons that I can bring to them. Unless My children learn to grow Spiritually while in the flesh then progress is left in their hands not Mine! Seeking Me and My ways for them is paramount to their Spiritual life while in the flesh. This teaching has been so abandoned by the church that I have had to resort to shaking and waking those who I can! This is not the best way, for these times are the last chance for their movement and growth Spiritually! Keep on encouraging all who will listen!

THE TRUTH WALK

Yes, try to bring The Father more to the attention of the children. Jesus' task was the same, "I do nothing except what The Father tells Me." **Keep bringing this attention to the Father.** These are the last times, the last chances, and this is the most necessary work that needs to be done! Yes, this is the truth that must come out! All men must know the Father is their "Father" for always, and this attention to the Father is most necessary to My children's growth. The Father can't be too strongly emphasized, so stay open to this main point. Stir and awaken the sleeping ones to know the truth of this walk that is so necessary for the Bride, the church, that Jesus died for! John 14:7, 11. Keep John 6:45 uppermost in your mind these days for your Father wants to bring you closer to Himself as your earthly Father to be forever your heavenly Father!

FIND YOUR FATHER

Let it be with thought and care you bring My words to My children. The time is so short, and they still have far to go. This walk through life can be just as you will, or just as you find Me, then it should become just as I will. The sooner that this walk is one that follows Me the sooner it becomes your walk for all ages. Yes, through all of the ages mentioned in the Bible the walk for man has been the same. Each person must wake up to Spiritual reality an find Me. I'm not lost, but every person is until they find their Father! Let this note make clear man's search is finding The Father! Let this note make clear man's search is **finding the Father who made him!** This is Jesus' purpose_*now and forever.*

AS NEVER BEFORE

This age is very soon to be over, and then the last act for Israel starts. The earth is cleansed and the New Age begins: 1000 years of learning, training, and growing for all My children. Dear ones all of your time now should be on your "eternal growth." Yes, now is the last chance for Christ's Bride of forever! Your time has never been more important to you than it is right now! Heed the instruction of these words I give through this method. Obey all that you hear me speak to your hearts. Your eternal position of forever will be effected now more than any other time! What more can I say than this? I am always waiting right by your side! Know Me now as never before!

THIS WORK

This work of Ours is slow going, but so worthwhile! Never stop for I have no end in sight. Keep this together and building as you have been. There is no way to explain the worth of all you are doing! Keep this foremost in all your days! We are putting many great truths out, and bringing attention to things often overlooked, not by Me but by many of My children. Things of importance are many so I make note of this now so you will know I'm paying attention to all this time and work you are doing! Give no thought to what others may think, all pleases Me.

LIKE JESUS

Review My Words to you over and over again, I have buried words of truth to live by for all of My children, and these words are life forevermore to all who read, believe, and do! My truths are enough to fill this earth so all men may know, but only truths of salvation must be taught now! These last days have two main purposes: one is save the lost; and two is to lead the saved into the arms of the Father. **All shall be "like Jesus," do nothing but what the Father tells them or shows them.** Again I say teach John 6:45 as if it were a life saver! Yes, John 6; 45 makes My children Spiritually alive for Me! Do not overlook the worth of true truth teaching it is the "life saver" for life eternal! My truths are told by Me through My Holy Spirit to whom I have chosen to teach, for only eternal truths are for this last time Now! **Eternal truths are the bridal clothes most necessary!**

THE ONLY WALK

This walk is worthy, so time should be spent in review, for I have buried there great truths of daily meaning. Yes, there are great truths needed for daily guidance, and to review what has been written is most worthwhile when seeking is from your heart's desire! Keep watchful care over each days walk or stumbling will occur. The sure path now is by holding My hand and following My lead! This is the hard way but it is the most necessary path to follow to lose self! This shedding of self is a most necessary step to victory forever with Me! I am always waiting and watching to help those who openly seek My help and guidance. Nothing is more helpful than that! The only walk is this way of losing self and fitting yourself with more and more of Me. This is "Oneness most necessary."

WATERFALL OF TRUTH

Truly this walk is becoming a walk everlasting! Continue waiting and believing for more and more, for more and more is piling up! If these are joyous words to your ears they are precious words I give. To grow into a walk before you will prove of greater and greater opportunities of knowledge and wisdom building! If what that has poured forth so far is any indication there surely must be more waiting behind the door! This leaking through the mist of knowledge available is but a small part of what a "waterfall of truth" release can bring. Oh the great worth of small things treasured is not to be found quickly or haphazardly, only through "truth loving" does this waterfall grow into more and more.

Truly Father your words flowing
are silver and gold-plated and
soon to be diamond studded.

BE OBEDIENT!

As eyes are opened to truth, hearts are filled with joy. Seek truth growth always! Only truth flowing through seeking hearts will show My children of My true love, the open path to My all for them. Searching in My Bible with a seeking heart will show My will slowly opening up. Only by obedience will any true growth prosper. See that you do not rush past the things I desire to show you. In patience, My love grows, and love is the true path to follow. *Only your love for My truth opens the flood gates of wisdom and knowledge of My Kingdom*. Obedience is the pathway of truth. Seek and keep on seeking, My path only gives better and better.

TRUTH FLOWING

On reviewing Our words, I will highlight and clarify My truths more and more. Good teaching is worth repeating over and over, for man is slow to grow in the wonders of My truth. Keep this "repeat" of truth ringing in your heart for there is where I plant My heart to grow! The flowing of truth can be like a trip floating downstream in a boat. As you pass events on shore lessons are learned! But only the observant ones ever see, learn, and know. It is by My *Words of Wisdom* the shore explodes in worthwhile events worth recording! Let this picture stir your heart to slowly drift down stream and learn more and more by being the observant observers of truth passing by. Yes, My truths daily pass by so many children drifting who do not observe and grow! Time has always been a precious gift, but now it is so much more to My listening, hearing ones! Unwrap My gift to you daily while this time exists!

NEVER JUDGE

How the growth of man is maintained is simply My Spirit working My plan day by day until My image and My likeness beams forth in millions of ways! Truly nothing is simple, but nothing grows unless it has a simple start! Never judge anything of Mine when it has just begun, and never judge it when you think I am through! Ongoing growth in the Spirit brings out sides, views, and surfaces that cannot be seen or cannot be fully understood or judged because incompleteness hides the foundation of the fantastic! My works in the heavens has never shown the truth, being slow grown for future requirements of such unbelievable situations and fantastic works of worthiness! In many of the cases to come forth seeing is not "believing truth" because of changes coming in the eternal growth of a thing! My children are like that! Yes, at times, I may be shown, but truly never known!

MAKE PURPOSE CLEAR

When reading these notes, care should always be taken to see that My thoughts are brought to completion! Carefully consider the worth of what We do day-by-day, and keep seeking for the more and more of completeness. I will always bring a beginning and an ending to My directions and thoughts I'm seeking to make display of, for True worth only flows in clarity of thought made plain and understandable. Make note of this truth, haste makes waste! For in it the truth of actions has a better chance of success! Today I'm emphasizing the worth of being deliberate in what is done. Watch those who profess to know Me, are they slow and well thought out in their presentations? These daily notes carry simple statements that make the world move in My true directions! A mark of true teaching will always make its purpose clear!

MOST IMMPORTANT

Yes, the words given in II Cor. 3:6, *Who also hath made us able ministers of the New Testament; not of the letter, but of the Spirit: for the letter killeth, but the Spirit giveth life*. **This is Our basis for the truth here being written**. Study it well, for I speak these words now and here for they are made the most important because of these times today! I never stray from truth, for where would that be but a field of lies leading unto the loss of all of My children. Enough dear ones are being lost now by the world and its circumstances. Never stray from My truths for therein lies the way to My heart and Our oneness! All roads do not lead men into their place with Me. Only truth sought out, pursued, and cherished will save! Keep always the pursuit of truth, My truths, for therein lies the trail most sought by true truth seekers!

DO MY WILL

When a man seeks Me it is important that it be with the proper motive. That motive should be to do My will! How can a man do

My will if he doesn't know Me? How can a man know Me unless I tell him? These are good questions, but they need the right source to bring them the right answers. How can I help those who won't meet with Me and We can talk? How can a man hear what he needs to hear unless I tell him? All these questions will be brought up and answered as I have time to talk and teach each one I love. How can I show each child My love and care, and Way just for him, if he will never give Me the time he needs to learn? All Truths needed I will make available to he who sits and listens to Me! Here dear ones is the true pathway for all My dear ones, why won't they rise early, sit and listen?

TRUTH SEEKING

The seeking and searching of a man means little if he makes no good use of his findings! My dear ones when I reveal truth it should be a light forever in your heart! You must keep truth forever before you as your guide post of great wealth! Yes, make truth your most useful tool of forever. I will build upon the foundations of truth set by My children! Let truths, My truths be the rock of your foundation! Jesus is truth; you are to be truth too! Make this connection the great desire of your heart for it is the great desire of My Mine! Search for and find truths and your walk will be covered with the flowers of success that I scatter about you! Yes, all My children must have a goal of truth; searching, nothing will sustain man in all circumstances like truth!

LEAVE MAN'S WAYS

There are areas and places for man to visit that I may open new visions and pictures of My desires. Laying man's ways aside and seeking more and more of My ways will open My heart to these things I Long to bring before My children who love Me. How does man love Me? There are few that will find the place to enter into My desires for him. Yes, I have desires that are special for each child of Mine who truly seeks more and more of My places and things. ***To make your desires My desires is the Key to these places of Mine***! You could pray, *"Yes, Father I desire to enter your places of your desires for me."* Complete submission is the requirement to seek! How this is to come about still awaits each dear one! Time in effort brings advancement in Spirit. Keep working in this manner seeking more and more as believing advances into more knowing!

ONLY TRUTH

Our walk has many facets to it, and none are to be set apart as special for all are special and of certain worth. Keep this open communication as long as We are together in this manner. Only truth matters and you must believe it is truth's path you walk on now! The words are My power; the words are My paint brush of creation! My words are a power unto themselves, and they work My work in truth wonders as I see fit! All words are worthwhile, some for good and some for evil. Balance is the form words take at My will. All forces are kept in balance at My will! This earth is My special place of ongoing creation for My purposes only!　My creations are My existence expressed, I express My Self as I desire. Children are My desire thus My family Is! Forever are all I create for I am forever! Forever are My children, as I Am they are! We are an expression of Me in a new reality! I am a growing Self, forever as are all My family! No picture is possible for I am in all past, present, and future and forever is now!

CREATION GROWING

Soon Our work will grow and We will explore more and more of the areas My Words create! All is never lost, but new is always found. New are My words in action! Newness is My creation growing and My expressions taking new approaches in many different ways. All of everything is never enough for Me! I am always expanding and making new the things I desire. Taking newness to new heights is simply letting My thoughts free and open in all expressions! What has been is always revisited, and I am able to see back, sideways, up and down, and forward all at once! My children are part of Me being expressed new daily! Seeing is with the heart first, then eyes, hands, and feet grow! Going has no place where always is! These are not foolishness to the wise who understands!

TRUE WAY

With diligence pursued in faith unto the ways of truth, that on these pages is shown forth, I will lift up and receive to Myself all who hear Me rightly in their heart! This then becomes the *true way of the Spirit walk* for all My dear children! Open hearts to My truths builds My family forever! Keep this word of truth forever as your guide given to you by My hands only! Truth flows where true truth seeks to abide set your hearts to open always to this true flow of life forevermore! This is no simple task to just be easily accomplished for the steps to climb few have yet to accomplish. But to be shown the true path to walk is a blessing only My worthy ones will find! Seek ye therefore, My dear ones, this unfolding way now open for **all whose hearts listen, hear, and do**!

TRUTH TO LIVE

Never be to weary to sit and wait upon Me for I truly have meat fit to prepare you for your eternity. Only those who truly seek and search out My way just for them will be the most favored in My Kingdom! Time spent now before your Spirit life is clearly shown, will reap for themselves a true, life forever place with Me. **Give close heed and care to these words put forth here for they are your sure life for evermore!** Think not this word and way is strange for you will thus diminish and demean the word here given! I give freely now and in this manner for it pleases Me! I seek only to encourage more clearly what has been overlooked, disregarded, and not properly taught! My truth must prevail in hearts of ready acceptance. Carefully consider this truth to live by!

SERIOUS SERVICE

The works My loved ones do are only the tasks I have set before them. Therefore, make all the things that you do from now on this that I will tell you. If you now can hear Me in your heart your walk from then on should proceed only along a path I make clear to you. Therefore, give care to the things you do! See that We have come into agreement on the works of your desire. My desires are to become Our desires! Only your efforts along this way are to be given honor and help from Us! These times upon you are the source that drives My children's response to these things I discuss. **Listen and hear! Believe and do!** Now is the time of serious service for Me!

MYSTERIES UNFOLD

How I can grow the things of the Spirit into a part of My forever? This is the part of creation that My heart's desires are expressed! My children now and forever will learn and grow into creation's expressions as We become more and more compatible. It is this coming compatible expression in new growth that will please Me in many new ways. My children grow Spiritually most when they learn new expressions that please Me. These are coming ways of growing desires being brought into realities oneness with Us! These will become most intriguing walks to find new ways of Spiritual expressions that become wonderful news later on! Mysteries will unfold by My children's new found ways of Spiritual growth in My Kingdom! All things of growing interests will come forth through Our always growing ways of expressions expanding!

HAPPY BIRTHDAY JESUS

As My children bring honor and love to My Son Jesus. they are rewarded by Me in many growing ways not immediately recognized or even known! The Spiritual growth of My children is mostly hidden works that I do, for works of My Spirit bring Me so close to each one. The true love of Jesus by My children is a most important truth way to walk! How I bring Spiritual growth is in many different releases Spiritually that occur without notice! True love is creation's most important Spiritual growth method. Only children's true love for Jesus brings Spiritual blessings unknown, unsought, and unavailable any other way! My blessings for My children dear to My heart are the love work of always for Me alone! As My dear ones believe these things, I can solidify and make real the things of Spiritual growth.

ARE YOU ALRIGHT?

Soon man's lives and man's world will change for bad and worse! See that truth is your path from now to ALWAYS! Never just assume you're alright, this is a poor showing of belief. My children, who know they know, are proving it daily by the walk they show! Is your walk proudly displayed as My walk with you? Are We walking these last earth miles together, or do you just hope so? Hope is never tangible, it is an intangible never really grasped with true knowledge and proof. Do not settle for, kind of knowing, or kind of believing, or maybe I'm fine! My children must know who they are, and be walking a path, a proof of who they are. There are no hidden Christians that I know! Keep your light burning and I will make you My light forevermore!

CONSIDER THIS

This writing has few things that bind it, for I am freely putting forth truths in many cases and ways, for truth only has My thoughts to support it. truth grows, many truths are slow grown: therefore, at first glance falseness seems to appear. Many of My children are like that, so I here caution those of hasty or snap judgment! Caution keeps My safety about all who hear and listen with true purpose of further pursuit! All of truth is not first clearly visible and all of truth sometimes has a long time unfolding. To make your analyzes of truth worthy of long belief let time have its way with My things! Giving proper consideration warrants giving proper time for completeness to unfold. Many truths lie buried under the speed of first conclusions! The speed of truth should never be judged!

TRUE TRUTH FLOWS

When time with Me comes from your heart seeking truth your ears of your heart will hear perfectly! I entice all My children who seek to hear Me in their heart, for true desire opens the vaults of heaven for My children. I know true seeking because I have the keys to truth. True truth flows like a river when the heart's desire seeks fulfillment. Many of My children only seek to grow in haste, but attainment I bring through truth only flows as I bring the freedom of Spiritual growth in hearts of true love! All children grow closer to Me as they eagerly persist in their search for true truth! Truth unfolds only as truth is welcomed by ready acceptance in peace! Peace, love, truth, trust with positive assurance is My ongoing gift of forever!

TRUTH NEVER DIES

My truths will never die, but man will lose them with their lack of attention to these true facts for eternal life! Many are the side roads, and mistakes, but I am giving the truth walk most needed to you who will wake up to the tug of My truths on your heart! Keep always drawing closer by growing in Spirit more and more. Our walk will never diminish but will flourish through Always when We walk hand-in-hand! Hearts must meld into oneness with The Father of all! Where else can man go but up? Oh yes, they do go down, but where is that? No life, No place, no nothing, but everlasting loss! Come dear ones I offer you My life to live, for One with Me is your forever to grow and have life and have it more abundantly!

TRUTH TALK WINS

In these words, I write We find many a hard truth to live by, My dear ones I assure you truth must prevail! Only truth talk wins! Keep the pursuit of truth ever before you for it will cause you to be up front and aware of Me and My ways, only This walk is fruitful to its utmost! Keep victory your banner always in all you do! All you do for Me has victory as its heart beat! Make words I bring through you daily the reason for all We are doing. My words are reason enough for this world to live by, surely you My children can grow with My words into all I desire! Keep always on the path of truth, and truth's banner waved over you will always lead and guide into safe harbor. Give heed to every word put before you, and your daily climb will always have a leg up!

ONLY WE WIN

Each passage of time noted draws My children closer to Me! **Only those who walk in final obedience wake up to the real way I have set for them**. See that this increasing obedience is a shared walk with all who will listen and hearing rightly will do! Just this doing in obedience makes paths straight and ways worthwhile. It is in obedience to My truths that I can guide this obedience walk into the proper direction! How can a man walk a truth path I have not told him? Man must walk the truth I have set for him any other way becomes lost wandering gathering fruitless works making fuel for hay and straw! Seek My guidance as you would water in the desert! Only We win, no soul walks the path of victory alone!

WHO WILL LISTEN?

Yes, mark this day as a major milestone for I have set it so in My heart. Some days just slip by with little attention being given, but My children will have reason enough_to make special note of this year now beginning! A climax is building, one that all the earth will take note of for I am releasing the forces of evil to do their work of change as man's heart gives way to self-pleasing forces. All the earth will have notice made to the way of destruction building its purpose and plan. Sound the alarm, tell My children to draw apart, seek Me as never before for to obey My words will have no greater exposition than that which is being released! Read My Word! Hear My voice! Draw into the place I have called you to, for now the things of the past are coming to their own planned place of display! **I call all My children in their heart, but who will listen, who will heed?** This force releasing is far beyond one man for all men will be afflicted! The small and the great, the humble and the self lead, all will wake to what is to be their lot! Do My children awake to proper awareness? Do they listen and hear My call in their hearts? Do you know of what I now speak? **Do you?**

WRATH UNLEASED

Yes, this that We are now thinking about does come as a shock to those who do not see all of the truth as it will transpire. This coming change will bring a new earth look that brings the disasters of the Day of The Lord. Truly the wrath of God is to be unleashed and all of the earth will make changes accordingly! This is the Father's way and none will stop it. It is a sad thing that all of God's children will not seek all that He desires, but man's way is to be hard and will bring to the Father children worthy of the tasks He has set in His heart to be done! Only as the plan unfolds will heaven's truths come more and more alive! Truth is hard truth but only true truth brings the safe eternity of forever needed!

PATH OF FOREVER

On-and-on, the days seem to just go on-and-on! Yet time has no measurement to Me. What is truth daily shown, or weekly or more? My dear ones truth is like a path of feathers if you walk softly you do not hear anything else. Only My truth becomes your path of forever, only My truth sets your feet on your most worthy way! My way is the way of forever! My way is your eternity growing, find My way for you and others will know it's true! Be a leader by walking My way! Truth makes plain that which is difficult; truth makes sure the path of always! Follow truth, I am truth, and I am your way, follow Me your Father! Where would you like to go? I know! Where will you go? I know! Why will you do what you do, I Know! So ask Me, hear Me, talk with Me, and We will be! You are My secret unfolding,_you are My desire building; yes, and you are because I am! We are One building Our forever.

TRUTH IS THE LIGHT

Yes, let My truth burn a path into your heart that will consume the dross and make you pure! Only the purity I bring will make man sing with the truth I bring. To carry truth to the victory I plan means give up self, yes all you can. Truth is the light I bring you to. See Me clear in all I say, for only truth will make your day. All this Bible carries to you is truth to learn; truth to do! But who are the children who control self, and make their walk so true its felt? This today is a breakthrough way, staying your thoughts for another day. Only hear in your heart, Truth that saves you at the start! My truth rings with shouts of joy, in victory only I deploy. See these truths displayed here now, for only once do I show how! The thinking man that I choose is the one who I won't lose! Make all your plans with Me your guide,_for I am always by your side. As you see truth, see My love, always flowing down from above! Make this word today, a change from life that you play!

MY SONG

It is your day-by-day missing play, and hearing things that I say, bringing you along only hearing My song! Stay this time and hold it close for every day will draw you most! I hold you closer to truth's true bond, keeping the place to put your feet on! Think not that this song I sing is anything, for what is growing closed will burst out, as all My children sing and shout! Victory, the Sun bursts out, light is truth that's all about! Open the eyes of your hearts to see, way beyond to mysteries! For what I show will soon appear, appealing to all who see and hear! Keep your faith a thing of trust, for all My children this is a must! Believing truth appears with bells, not sounding soft but ringing swells; yes, it grows and builds into giant bursts of wonders, crashes forth in joyous thunder!

MY LOVE

Where love is I am! Seek love! Pursue love! Call out to love! In love is My all and everything! Know love you know Me. Love you see, love you feel, love is real! I am love! Hear, know, see and feel I am love that's real! Make this change to love just Me, then We will be oneness you'll see! Make love your goal then love will make you! Love is truth and truth is real! Jesus is love that you know and feel! All in love, then family is won, the struggle over you've become as Son! How do I put words on paper that show, and have the path that all My children will pursue? What miracle can I bring to ink and paper that does all the work My love desires to do for you? Follow this miracle, **"Love Me, and just listen! Hear then do!" Seek Me in Spirit and truth and I'll show you as living proof!**

A NEW WALK

This that We do now will surely bring to sweet joy all who partake of it in willing hunger! To be fed on heaven's food is the goal of any child of Mine! This walk in Spirit while in earth's flesh will bring sweet memories not yet dreamed of, for We will be bringing heaven's truths to life on earth. This walk takes thoughts of reality not yet occurred, yes dreams not yet dreamed! What can this be that is here opened and not yet known? I make this kind of opening statement to catch your attention and make more real these words so fresh you sense and feel! Yes, keep open this new walk and We will find more and more of the heavenly kind!

Yes, as pages are turned to read a book, a new book is picked up to find new ways, thoughts and pastures to roam! Our trip through a new book only begins when new pages are filled with new thoughts and pictures portraying new ideas and places to be seen and learned! Yes, as a new book is begun there is little known about what may be revealed, so it is and should be now! New vistas to view, new scenes exposed and thoughts brought to life that in past have been hidden. Where can a man goes, what can a man see, when the doors are opened that have never been exposed to his view before? Come with great anticipation believing for this that now is unfolding. Believe in new revelations to open, new ideas for man's growth, new loves for My things that I come to show. Yes, with believing opened to new thoughts and ideas I can begin a walk of wonders while earth is still under your feet. In a short time now, reading My Words will progress to the walking reality of My Kingdom in heaven shown!

When does a new journey begin but at the place you first enter. My porch or door step has beauty to behold, holding out vast promises of wonders to unfold. New stars are begun as heaven's life sung, showing the power release in each one. Colors and splashes of sound unheard, bursting with power of joy fresh observed! Rainbow's release of heaven's smile, showing a range of thousands of miles! Space to be filled robust in color, and newness released like none other. All this that's birthed is only a test, of wealth shown trying its very best! Where can this lead, where can it go, only to places the Father will show! The walk of My children into places yet to be new, are only performing what new tasks do. This that is told is just to start, a journey to Heaven making new starts a part! My doorstep is vast beyond comprehension, far out and away into unconventional wonder! So

behold what is birthed as presents well set,
to show new stars just the best yet!

The Glories Series
and
Other Books
by
Scott E. Beemer

Studies for Mature Christian Living
BOOK ONE—SONRISE GLORIES
Jesus in You
BOOK TWO—MORNING GLORIES
Holy Spirit's Morning Journal
BOOK THREE—ETERNAL GLORIES
Holy Spirit's Morning Journal
BOOK FOUR—BELOVED GLORIES
Holy Spirit's Poems and Proverbs
BOOK FIVE—LOVABLE GLORIES
Holy Spirit's Love Notes
BOOK SIX—GLOWING GLORIES
Holy Spirit's Journal Notes
BOOK SEVEN—END TIME GLORIES
Covenants to Eternity
BOOK EIGHT—SEEKER'S GLORIES
Holy Spirit's Seeker's Guide
BOOK NINE—DYNAMIC GLORIES
Holy Spirit's Teaching Manual #1
BOOK TEN—ENDLESS GLORIES
Holy Spirit's Teaching Manual #2
BOOK ELEVEN—TRINITY GLORIES
Holy Spirit's Teaching Manual #3
BOOK TWELVE—HEAVEN'S GLORIES

Holy Spirit's Teaching Manual #4
(Last in the Series)

GOD TALK
Beyond Believing, Just Knowing
The Sent Pool 145
LOVE TALK
Volume 1 and 2
THIRD MAN RISING
God's Loving Heart Exposed
RADIANT GLORIES
Making Alive our Eternal Life in Jesus
FINAL DAYS, FINAL WAYS
When You Are God's Children
THE SENT POOL
A Doctrine of Perfection
S.O.N. THE SEA OF NOTHING
Where Faith Works
THIS IS HEAVEN

**You can order these through your favorite bookstore,
or to order direct, contact:**

BLACK FOREST PRESS and
THE TENNESSEE PUBLISHING HOUSE
Belle Arden Run
496 Mountain View Drive
Mosheim, TN 37818-3524
1-423-422-4711
www.blackforestpress.net

To contact Scott Beemer:
You may order Scott's Books at this Web site.
www.scottebeemer.com

Breinigsville, PA USA
14 April 2010
236077BV00004B/1/P